For Earl — my rock.

And for Ben,
the best brother a sister could have.

Thrive

The Entrepreneurial Path
to a Great Life

Robin A. Sheerer

Thrive: The Entrepreneurial Path to a Great Life
by Robin Sheerer

©Copyright 2012

ISBN-13: 978-1475284478

Author Website:
http://www.careerenterprisesinc.com/

Email:
careerenterprises@gmail.com

Printed in U.S.A.

Also by Robin Sheerer
No More Blue Mondays:Four Keys to Finding Fulfillment at Work
(Gold Medal Benjamin Franklin Award Winner for Best Career Book of the Year, 2000)

Cover and Interior Design:
http://RelentlesslyCreative.com

Contents

Part III. Learn the Art of Thriving

Still on Fire (A Conclusion)

Part IV: Suggested Exercises and Action Steps

Gratitude

Fired Up
(An Introduction)

Jane and John strolled into their first appointment with me as their career coach looking relaxed and clearly in love. Although both wore jeans, they presented a contrast: she with blond, spiky hair and a sophisticated lambs wool vest and he with a crew cut, nerdy glasses, and a baseball cap. They had come to redesign their individual futures and because they were blending their lives, had decided to talk about it as a couple.

In their fifties, they had worked for many years out of expediency rather than passion. John had spent years in manufacturing and Jane in operations. Now they were eager to pursue a path that would allow them to do work they loved and also have a great lifestyle. Jane wanted to be more creative. John wanted to give back after many years of success. They both wanted work that would allow them to contribute to others and still have time for fun together.

By the end of that meeting, they agreed that their best chance to fulfill their dreams was to pursue independent entrepreneurial paths. They left full of ideas and ready to get into action. (Read more about Jane later in this book). I couldn't help thinking, there's nothing like an inspiring vision to wake you up and get the juices going.

Whether you're young or old, I'm convinced an entrepreneurial path is your best chance to have both work and a life you love. It's your best chance whether you're brand new to starting a business or you're in the process of redesigning the one you've had for twenty years. Because you're reading this, I bet you agree with me.

If you're hesitating because of doubts and fears, I understand totally. I haven't forgotten what it was like in 1981, over thirty years ago, when I quit a salaried job to work full time in my own business offering career and professional development coaching, consulting, and training. I was forty-one years old and just like today, we were in a deep recession. I was scared to death. At the same time, I was passionate, excited, and fiercely determined. In short, I felt fully alive. It was one of the best times in my life.

I can assure you that if I've been able to do it, you can too. When I started, I didn't know the first thing about what I was doing so I've poured everything I've learned into this book to help you get off to a great start, learn how to handle tough times, stick with it for the long haul, and stay true to yourself in the process.

Initially I thought I wanted to build a big business on a national level but I discovered that a small business fits me well. I've loved my work and am glad I made the choices I did.

This book is perfect for you if you want a business ranging in size from one (you) to about twenty employees, if you're willing to give up more income for more time with your family and friends, if you're happy earning "enough" and don't want to amass a fortune, if you're more interested in quality than quantity, and if you prefer remaining close to your business and clients instead of building an empire. Even if you intend to grow your business, you need to build a firm foundation first and the issues, challenges, and principles included in this book will apply to you.

Over twenty-five years ago I created monthly support groups for my entrepreneurial clients. Facilitating them all these years has given me the unique opportunity to become intimately familiar with what entrepreneurs face on a day-to-day basis. In our meetings we never lose sight of the importance of thriving in business *and* personal life. Many of these clients' stories are in my book, as well as my own. They're all true. I've only made changes to protect privacy.

Starting a business is a career decision and it's important to make sure that it's a good fit for you, that the time is right, and that you have the fire in your belly to make it happen. I'll help you think all that out in Part I. Ultimately, it comes down to making a commitment and putting a stake in the ground, but you don't have to scare yourself to death like I did. There are sane ways to do it. Still, it takes a leap of faith and courage. If you're lucky, you'll be someone who knows you can't *not* do it.

You are the heart and soul of your business and how you manage yourself is the real bottom line. In Part II, you'll find powerful practices you can incorporate to survive and build momentum, help with thinking through the decisions that can have a big impact on your business and your life, and advice about money, the one area that makes most people nutty.

If you've been self-employed for a while, there's the danger of falling into a rut and allowing your business to turn into a job. Before you know it, you're complaining again, just like when you were employed. In Part III, you'll read about how to keep your business vital over the long haul, take good care of yourself, stay in touch with your passion, continue to express yourself authentically, and reinvent yourself as needed while remaining an entrepreneur.

I've included exercises and action steps in Part IV. I promise you they're not just "busywork" and urge you to do them.

In my eyes, anyone who starts from scratch and builds something out of nothing is a hero or heroine. I know what it takes to get a business up and running and keep it going. So this book is written for all of you who are entrepreneurs already, and for those of you who will be, with my wishes for a vibrant business *and* a life you love for as many years as you want to work.

A blessing, as you start this book:

"May you have the courage to listen to the voice of desire
that disturbs you when you have settled for something safe."

—from *To Bless the Space Between Us* by John O'Donohue

Robin Sheerer

Spring, 2012

Please note: I've used the terms self-employed, small business owner, and entrepreneur interchangeably throughout the book.

Part I
Design Work and a Life You Love

Chapter 1
Trust Yourself

Everyone thinks you'd be crazy to leave the safety and security of a job to leap into self-employment. Well, okay, mainly it's your mother. Recently, in the middle of telling her about your business idea, she interrupted and asked in that familiar worried voice, "But darling, why in the world would you leave such a good paying job for an uncertain future?" Startled, you held the phone away from your ear and stared at it in awe. It was like listening to the self-doubts in your own head.

It's easy to give up on your dreams after a conversation like this with a family member, coworker, or friend, but it can even happen with a stranger. It almost stopped my client Angie in her tracks.

"I feel isolated and vulnerable in my job," she complained

at our first meeting. "A year ago, I got a new boss. He demands I justify everything and totally dismisses my skills. Even though he promoted me to Director, he leaves me out of important meetings and doesn't even answer my emails."

After thirty years of experience as a career and professional development coach, I recognized the signs of an imminent lay-off. "Uh oh. Sounds like the handwriting is on the wall," I told her.

Just as I thought, Angie's job was eliminated shortly after that session. Although her boss suggested other opportunities inside the organization, Angie asked herself, "Is this what I want to do?" Her answer was a definite "no." At age forty-nine, after twenty years with the company, she negotiated a settlement and left with no idea what to do next.

She gave herself time to grieve and let go of her job and then weeks later, announced in a flat tone of voice that she thought she should return to working inside a corporation.

"Well, you certainly don't sound happy about it," I said. Knowing from experience that people often have dreams buried deep inside, I asked, "What do you really want to do? What could you get excited about?" Hesitantly, she answered that when she was young she had loved running the cash register in her father's pharmacy and had dreamt about having a store since then.

You should have seen her as she talked about it. She leaned forward in her chair, and her eyes sparkled. It looked like this might be the right direction for her, but at our next appointment she surprised me by backing off.

"It's too risky," she announced. The same person who had been enthusiastic just two weeks ago now sat slumped in her chair, her voice weak, and her eyes brimming with tears.

I smelled a rat. I suspected she'd had a demoralizing conversation with someone in between our appointments. "What happened?" I asked. Sure enough, she had met an exhausted, cranky retailer who questioned her sanity, told her it would be a big mistake to open a store, and advised, "Just forget about it. Get a job." Now she doubted her dream and reported she had spent the past week rewriting her resume to begin a job search.

"Is that what you really want?" I asked.

"I guess so. It would be okay," she answered in a desultory voice. I groaned. Okay was not good enough. Before I could reply, she added, "But my heart isn't in it."

Ah, heart, the repository of our dreams and our soul's deepest longings. This was the crux of the matter. If she nurtured and protected her dreams until she grounded them in reality, Angie's heart could lead her to an enlivening and vibrant future. But if she listened instead to internal voices that told her what she "should" do, she would settle for an inauthentic life. She would leave the most important part of herself out of the equation. I hoped she would have the strength to honor her heart's desire.

17

Doubts and fears can be formidable adversaries though. I remember a meeting with Margaret. We had met at Ina's, a favorite restaurant located on the near west side of Chicago with a cozy atmosphere and comfort food. She had requested an opportunity to network and because we were new to each other, filled me in on her work history as I munched on curried chicken salad and grainy bread. A few months ago she had left a fifteen-year stint as an executive with a Fortune 100 company. She leaned over the table and whispered, "If I could have my ideal life, I'd offer coaching to a small group of clients and work with several people inside companies to help them develop leadership skills. And I'd teach a course and write."

Whispering? What was with that?

You have probably already guessed that I immediately asked, "Well, why don't you?" She slumped back in her chair, recited a long list of fears, and stated in a weak voice that she didn't know how to get started.

Knowing that if you get busy and fuel your dreams, doubts and fears will diminish, I suggested, "You have everything you need to do it. Just start by getting two clients."

With only that tiny bit of encouragement, her energy rose like the steam from her coffee cup. She sat up straight, and said in a full voice, "Well, I can do that. What a relief not to have to figure it all out at once."

Are you surprised to learn that both Margaret and Angie managed complex projects in their prior jobs? Everyone who considers stepping away from being employed has doubts and fears; it has nothing to do with position, talent, and ability. Even if you were a leader in your prior position, you will enter the unknown as an entrepreneur. And that's both exciting and scary for everybody.

When you're self-employed, everything depends on you, at least initially. If you're not buying an existing business or a franchise, you have to make everything up from scratch every single day — what product or service you'll offer, how much it will cost to do it, what you should charge, who your potential clients or customers are, how to reach them, and how to structure the business. You'll have to generate enough money to pay business and personal expenses. Most entrepreneurs thrive on this challenge but it takes courage to step away from company perks — paid sick days and vacation, matched 401 contributions, health insurance, administrative support, colleagues and friends, an office, maybe even a company car. Is your mind going into overdrive?

"What if I can't make enough money?" you wail.

Calmly, I reply: "Most of my clients and entrepreneurial friends do as well, or better, than they did when they were employed. The world is full of opportunities. Just open your eyes."

Certain this will be a deal breaker, you challenge, "But what about health care?"

Still calm, I answer, "You'll find a solution. All my clients do, even those who have spouses who are also self-employed."

Then you present what you consider to be the pièce de résistance:

"What if I never find such brilliant, wonderful co-workers again?"

No longer calm, I respond: "C'mon. Get real. The world is full of great people. Just open your heart."

"Okay," you say to me. "I get that, but...."

"Oh boy, here we go again. I bet you had another conversation with your mother."

"Yep, and this time she asked in a sweet voice, 'But is it a real job?'"

I remember when my client John asked me that same question. When I met him he was miserable working as a CPA in a large accounting firm. He had reached the point where he knew it wasn't right for him but didn't know what else to do.

"Out of all your past accomplishments, which ones did you find deeply satisfying and fulfilling?" I asked in one of our meetings. There was a dramatic change in him as he told me about rehabbing apartments in his spare time and then selling them for a profit.

"You're excited when you talk about this. Why haven't you thought about doing this as your work?" I asked.

"It's just a hobby. Well, I loved it and made good money, but I don't know if I can make enough to support my family. Besides, it's not real work is it? It's not a corporate job."

I sighed. "John, you've put corporate America on too high a pedestal. There are plenty of other ways to have a great career. I bet a thriving underground of self-employed people lives right in your neighborhood." I told him to look around. "They're in business dress, jeans, or sweats drinking coffee and eating in cafes or nearby restaurants while working on laptops or iPads. All of them are supporting themselves and contributing to our economy."

After that meeting John talked about his idea with his wife, explored real estate development, and left his job. Since then, he's renovated apartments, converted units to condos or kept them as rentals, and has built and sold several houses. Even in this current recession when the real estate market has suffered huge losses, John has been flexible and has found ways to keep his business going.

And what did Angie decide? At our next meeting, she surprised me by bringing a notebook bulging with pictures of products she would carry if she had a store. She confessed she'd been working on it for three years. Well, now. This story is not over yet, I thought. This was a clue to a passion if I ever saw one.

Angie's bad experience with a negative retailer underscores an important lesson: don't share your dream with curmudgeons.

21

Learning to survive as a small business owner begins the moment you recognize you have a dream. Because dreams are fragile in the early stages, avoid sharing with people who are discouraging and feed your fear. This includes your mother. Wait until she becomes your biggest fan, or until you feel so strong nothing will stop you.

In the meantime, keep your enthusiasm high by fueling your intention. Read motivational books about your business idea. Like Angie did, collect pictures to serve as a vivid reminder. Attend classes, workshops and conferences, or join professional organizations to build a body of knowledge and a network of like-minded people.

Can I guarantee you'll be successful if you take the leap? No. You can't control all the factors that might impact you — world events, the stock market, competition, the rise and fall of fads. But I'm convinced that 90% of being successful with a small business depends on a good fit and how you manage yourself. These you can control and I'll help you with both.

Here's what I do guarantee: if you take the leap, you'll be excited and enlivened. Your life will be enriched. And even if the outcome doesn't meet the pictures you envisioned, you'll expand your skills and experience and gain depth as a human being. You'll be a bigger person because you allowed yourself to pursue a dream. I'm confident about this because I've learned from working with thousands of people that our hearts are trustworthy guides.

If, like Angie, you have a dream, protect it.

If, like Margaret, you have an idea, hold fast to it.

If, like John, you have a passion, take it seriously.

Most of all, trust yourself. It's the first step on the path to a great life.

Chapter 2
Tap into Your Fierce Desires

We chose to meet at the East Bank Club, a glitzy fitness center nestled along the Chicago River. Kelly was a new friend and we were having a great time getting to know each other. We confessed that we both loved breakfast and ordered way too much food, including mango apricot bread. Who could resist? Not me.

She was tiny and her silky black shoulder-length hair swung as she talked animatedly. I discovered she was only forty years old and had been on her own as a management consultant for eight years already.

"I can't imagine being brave enough to start a business at thirty-two. You've done really well," I said, referring to her list of impressive clients.

"Yes, this past year's been especially good," she acknowledged.

Then without missing a beat, she added, "But nothing's happening right now. Next year could be another great year or a blank calendar." Fear had just joined us as a third guest at the table and the mood altered abruptly. She paused and then knowing I was a seasoned entrepreneur asked, "Does the fear ever go away?"

For a moment I was tempted to lie but I know that all entrepreneurs have doubts and fears some of the time, most of the time, or all of the time, either on loudspeaker or as a low hum in the background. Fear has been present for me so often over my years of being self-employed I consider it a close family member. I told the truth: "No, it never disappears. You learn to handle it or you decide not to work on your own."

"That's what I thought," she said. Sighing, she shrugged her shoulders and dug into her food again. By the end of our meal I was confident she'd continue to thrive but probably not for the reason you think. It wasn't her solid background or even her great track record. I knew she'd be fine the moment she told me she cared more about being on her own than having the security of a paycheck. She had the single most important ingredient that motivates every successful entrepreneur I know — a fierce desire for freedom. It trumps fear every time.

In Chicago-speak, ya gotta' wanta.' When I stepped out on my own in 1981 at the age of forty-one, gripped by the desire for freedom, I declared, "I never want to work for anyone ever again, unless I have to." It's still my guiding mantra.

Everyone whines, sulks, or complains about work from time to time. It's not a problem unless it becomes a way of life and you begin to feel and act like a victim. If that happens, then it's time to look deep inside, be honest, and take action. If the truth is that you want to remain employed, then turn things around by transforming your complaints into clear requests and deliver them to the right people. On the other hand, if the truth is that you hate being employed and yearn to live and work on your own terms, then stop whining and get to work on creating a business. Just make sure one or more of the following five fierce desires for freedom motivates you:

1. To be your own boss

2. To do the work you want to do

3. To design your life the way you want it to be

4. To express yourself more creatively

5. To make as much money as you can through your own efforts.

Are you motivated by a fierce desire to be your own boss? Are you someone who doesn't like to be told what to do? Do you want to make your own decisions, be in charge, and call the shots? Do you welcome being responsible for all of it? After being self-employed for over sixteen years, one of my clients put it well when she declared, "I'm completely unemployable now." She loves being self-reliant and could never return to having a boss again and a friend who's been an entrepreneur for over thirty years confessed that whenever he pictures himself working for a company, he knows the first time someone said something stupid, he'd be out of there.

Some of my clients wandered from job to job or were fired repeatedly before they discovered their strength was in being self-employed, but you don't have to be a rebel to succeed (although it helps). Maybe you're like some entrepreneurs who were leaders inside companies and good corporate citizens before they stepped out on their own. Regardless of your work history, if you have strong opinions about how you think things should be done, it would not surprise me to discover that you're a perfectionist. Many entrepreneurs are. If you're quiet, even introverted, or a wild extrovert who thrives on being social, it doesn't matter, as long as you're determined to be your own boss.

Do you have a fierce desire to do the work you want to do? Do you resent having to do work that doesn't interest you? As a business owner, you won't mind working hard. In fact, you'll enjoy it because you're pursuing interests and passions. And best of all, you're getting paid for it: writing, cooking, leading workshops or giving speeches, consulting with people in business, inventing and selling products, teaching, creating videos, healing people, or designing advertising and marketing campaigns. You can work for hours and hours without getting tired or bored. To quote one entrepreneur, "I'm working really, really hard, but it's fine because I'm doing what I love."

Do you have a fierce desire to design your life the way you want it to be? Would you cherish the flexibility to plan work around your life, instead of your life around work? Would you love being able to spend time with your children, attend their activities, get them off in the morning, and be home when they return from school? The owner of a small publishing company told me, "I'm slow to wake up in the morning, so that's when I sit with my coffee and read. Later in the day, I perk up and have a lot of energy. I work hard until my kids come home from school. Then I get a second wind after they go to bed and I work late into the evening. I love it. It suits my rhythms." Maybe you want to take seriously long vacations rather than work harder to make more money, or exercise regularly, or take classes that interest you in art, photography, or history. Maybe you long to volunteer and be involved in your community. The bottom line is that you yearn for a whole life that's rich and varied and not consumed entirely by work. You want to be able to say, as one of my clients did, "I have my life back."

Do you have *a fierce desire to express yourself more creatively?* Do you have strong right-brain skills (relationship building, designing, big picture thinking, etc.) that are not utilized or appreciated in your current job? Do you feel like a fish out of water in a company that depends on left-brain skills (linear thinking, attention to details, analysis, etc.)? Perhaps you're longing to be inventive, work with people instead of technology, and use your design or artistic skills more fully. Do you thrive on being creative and have a fierce desire to be authentic and express yourself? This is a perfect time for you according to author Daniel Pink who writes in *A Whole New Mind*: "The future belongs to a different kind of person.... creative and empathetic right-brain thinkers whose abilities mark the fault line between who gets ahead and who doesn't."

Do you have a *fierce desire to make as much money as you can through your own efforts*? Have you felt overlooked in the workplace or were you told outright that you'd never get the position you wanted? Or are you frustrated and discouraged knowing that no matter how hard you work your income will always be limited by a ceiling set by someone else? Are you motivated by the thought that the sky is the limit and your earnings will depend on your own efforts? Just don't go into business based solely on a desire to make money. As author Tal Ben-Shahar, a Harvard professor, writes in his book entitled *Happier*, "Happiness, not gold or prestige, is the ultimate currency." So carefully choose work you love and turn that into a thriving business, like my client Gary did.

Gary's fifty-fifth birthday triggered a wish to act on his

dream to be self-employed. He left a position as Vice President
of Marketing in a Fortune 500 company because he no longer
was willing to work sixty-hour weeks and did not want to take on
more responsibility knowing he would have to put in even more
hours. Instead, he wanted to focus his time and energy on coaching people to be more effective in the area he loved – business
development. With thirty years of experience under his belt, he
was confident he could better serve clients and also have a different lifestyle that would allow him to work less, spend more time
with his family, become more physically active and fit, and earn
more income.

He networked for months before he left the company and
lined up several contracts. Now on his own, he works four days
a week doing work he loves and earns twice as much as when he
was employed full time. He's lost forty-five pounds and his physical strength has improved. Last summer he and his wife participated in a five hundred mile bike ride. He has a home office and
more free time than he has had in years. His biggest challenge is
saying no to all the opportunity in front of him.

Self-employed people get up in the morning and start work
without anyone telling them what to do. They're passionate about
being on their own and if they choose carefully, they also love the
work they do. They use their talents fully. They design lifestyles
to avoid energy-draining commutes. They express their creativity.

They're motivated by the thought that their earnings are capped only by their own efforts. The freedom bug has clearly bitten them. Once they leave employment, they rarely return to it.

Are you nodding your head and muttering, "Yep, that's me"? If you're still filled with doubts and fears, do you wonder if that means you shouldn't do it? Absolutely not. There's a thin line between fear and excitement and also between doubt and desire. It's a matter of where you put your focus. Shift your attention onto your excitement and let the energy of desire carry you forward.

Fierce desire is the fire in your belly that will empower you to jump from the known into the unknown. It will move you through doubts and fears over and over again, whenever they arise, especially if your freedom means more to you than anything else.

Chapter 3
Choose the Right Time

Beth looks terrific. She's in her mid-forties and has a strong, toned body without an ounce of extra fat. She's crazy about fitness, loves being outdoors, exercises regularly and vigorously, eats healthy foods, and whenever she can, rides her bike instead of driving a car.

Two months prior to meeting with me she had been let go as a partner in a large law firm where she had worked for ten years. Although she enjoyed business transactions, she had been unhappy for a long time. She complained about the way clients treated her and resented how much her work had bled into her personal life.

I was confident she could land another legal job on her own, so I was curious why she wanted to meet.

"I need to stay energized and focused because the job search is taking a while. Also, my husband and I are considering moving to a different climate so we can be outdoors more, but we don't know where. Maybe Colorado or California." Then, almost in passing, she added, "Maybe I should consider something entirely new. I've thought about starting a fitness center, or I might like to be a Pilates instructor, or a personal trainer. But that's probably far in the future. Maybe I'd be happier as an in-house general counsel, or in a smaller law firm. That might be interesting."

Whew. What a swirl of issues.

"Can you take some time to sort all this out?" I asked.

At first she insisted she needed to land work right away, but I encouraged her to slow down. She reviewed her finances, cut back on expenses, and negotiated an extension of her severance from the law firm. She began to relax and meet casually with people to network. A few weeks later, she was offered a temporary in-house counsel position filling in for a woman going on maternity leave in the fall. This was her chance to try on a new role and with that lined up, she enjoyed the rest of the summer spending time with her daughter, having lunch with her husband, playing tennis, teaching an exercise boot camp, and working out.

As summer began to wane and the smell of fall filled the air, Beth told me she was more committed than ever to examine the possibility of starting a business. "Health and fitness is all I talk about," she said.

I had my doubts. It didn't feel right when she talked about it. Something was missing. I couldn't put my finger on it but I wondered if she was committed enough to do what it takes to start a business. I questioned whether she would turn her back on all the years she had invested in practicing law, leave behind a substantial income (at least initially, maybe forever), start as a novice again, and reinvent herself. It would require a fierceness I hadn't felt yet.

In September, after beginning her temporary job, Beth emailed that she was in tears because she missed her family. She added, "The one thing that's a bright light is that I'm listening to personal fitness training CDs in the car on my long commute and I'm continuing to lead the Boot Camps." Still, I wasn't convinced that she'd be ready to start a business of her own after this temporary assignment ended.

Here's what ultimately happened. Once she adjusted to being back at work, she found the work challenging and interesting. The company turned out to be a good fit. She gave it everything she had. Her only complaint was the long commute.

"If they want me to stay and make the right offer, I'll take it," she told me. (They did, and she did). "And if they don't, I'll continue to look for a job as an in-house counsel. I'm not through with being a lawyer," she concluded. This powerful insight felt like the truth.

I think she made the right decision at this point in her life.

Even though she yearned for a different life-style, she wasn't done using her legal skills or with being employed. This was the "something" that I had sensed was missing.

It's become clear to me that the right time to become self-employed depends less on external factors than on being ready internally. Beth is an example of someone who was not ready. My client Dave, on the other hand, is an example of someone who was.

I was excited when he called for an appointment because I hadn't seen him for several years. He was even more handsome in his late forties than I remembered him, his dark black hair now lightly tinged by silver at the temples.

After reporting that he'd been let go recently from a job with a well-known national consulting firm, he explained he was finding it difficult to land the work he wanted in this tough economic environment. He confessed he'd been driven by money in his last several job choices and now he was determined to choose the next job for the right reasons.

"I don't want to grab a job out of panic," he stated. I promised him I'd stay on the side of his heart and help keep him grounded.

Over several weeks he turned up a couple of good job possibilities but, as often happens in the early stages of a job search, all of them evaporated. He decided he had to do something to generate income while he continued looking.

"I love coaching company leaders to grow successful businesses. I'm willing to tell them the truth," he said. Because this is rare around leaders, I knew he'd be greatly valued as a confidant and advisor. Here's the other clue that he was on the right path: as he talked about it, he lit up and his energy filled the room. Secretly, I hoped he'd decide to start his own consulting business but when I suggested it, he dismissed the idea, saying, "I don't want to do that. I did that for a while years ago and didn't like it."

Weeks later he began to panic with no job in sight, savings diminished, and college costs looming for two kids. Although I rarely encourage clients to pursue a job and start a business at the same time, this seemed like a good idea under the circumstances. Okay, I admit, it was a little sneaky on my part.

"Why don't you start doing what you want to do on your own right now? Then with clients landed, you'll have something extra to bring to the table when you're negotiating for a job," I suggested.

Dave had already created a unique audit for company leaders and after our conversation he began showing it to business contacts. Everyone gave him positive feedback that it was timely and needed. He decided to drop the job search and focus on building a business.

He was like a racehorse out of the gate. He created a Power

Point presentation and a web site, landed great PR, wrote a white paper, and networked with lots of people. To avoid being isolated and stay on track, he also joined a monthly support group for entrepreneurs that I facilitate.

"I think it's a business that will let me be the person I want to be. It combines my experience, passion, and a great market opportunity," he reported happily.

"What's different now from when you tried being self-employed before?" I asked.

"Last time I didn't like all the uncertainty around money and chasing contracts. Also, I didn't know how to pull the right people around me."

"And now?"

"I'm not the same guy I was ten years ago," he answered.

He was absolutely right. Now he was more experienced, smarter, and more mature. I was confident he would manage the uncertainties better and attract or find the people he needed.

"What about the money?" I asked.

"Oh, I can do better on my own," he asserted.

Dave had everything going for him to be successful, including the advantage that he was good at sales. "I think it's the right thing at the right time," he said. I agreed. Of course, he was also scared, impatient, and anxious, but I reminded him that it usually takes a while to get a business up and running.

In a matter of only a few months, Dave landed a lot of work. He never bought into fears about the slow economy. In fact, he was convinced his services were needed now more than ever. And, he had a fierce desire to pursue his passion.

Okay. This is a perfect time for you to take your own internal reading. Are you more like Beth or Dave? The answer doesn't matter; you just need to tell the truth. Is becoming an entrepreneur a powerful, motivating force within you, or just a good idea? Are you done with being employed? Do you feel ready regardless of circumstances surrounding you?

There's probably no such thing as the perfect time to start a business. External conditions are important, but internal readiness is crucial. When you're ready, the dream has you — you don't have it. You can't not do it. Some people label it stubbornness. I call it passion.

Don't look to the outside world for affirmation. If you have a product or service that's wanted or needed, you've let go of the past and are ready to create a new life, any time can be the right time to start a business.

Look inside.

Your intuition is your best guide.

Chapter 4
Be Sure it's a Good Fit

"What's going on? I hear through the grapevine that you're leaving your current job," I said to Barb. I had run into her while walking Molly, my erratically groomed Schnauzer who sat quietly next to me while we chatted (very effective behavior designed to ingratiate people and get petted).

"My uncle and I just purchased an oil change franchise and I'm going to run it," she said. Her answer left me uncharacteristically speechless, not because I doubted a woman could run an automotive-related business, but because the person who stood in front of me was dressed impeccably, had carefully styled hair, beautifully manicured nails, and a formal way of speaking. From seeing her in the neighborhood, I knew that even her dog was consistently well groomed. I couldn't picture her working eight or more hours a day in a plain tiny office housed in a smelly grease-filled garage, surrounded by young men whose major topics of conversation would be cars, sports, who they scored with, and how much they drank last night.

A few years later when I saw Barb again, she announced she'd closed the business because the location proved to be bad and they didn't have enough traffic. I've always secretly thought the problem was that it was a bad fit. Before buying the franchise, I wonder if she asked herself: Is this my kind of work? Will I look forward to coming here every day? Are these my kind of people? Is this a good fit for me? I think she was in love with the idea of having a business but not the business itself. Many people start businesses thinking it's enough that they just want to be an entrepreneur. It makes me want to tear my hair out.

After thirty years as a career and professional development coach, I'm convinced that a good fit is the single most important ingredient for happiness at work. What does that look like? It's a good fit if you experience ease and flow in your work. Not every minute. Not even every day. But if your work is so engrossing (and enjoyable) most of the time that you lose yourself in what you're doing, the hours fly by, and your aches, pains, worries, and to-do lists recede into the background, it's a good fit.

It's a good fit if your temperament matches your work. If the business is stressful and you're calm in a crisis, that's a good match. Or, if the business demands that you do solitary work and that's the way you prefer it, great. Just think about what feels natural to you.

If you will use your talents, skills, and abilities often, and your values will align with what you do, it will be a good fit. You'll never feel comfortable if you work outside your strengths or if you have a major conflict with values.

A good fit doesn't mean you won't work hard. It's just that you'll rarely consider it drudgery. If you enjoy it, and feel deeply satisfied and fulfilled at least 80% of the time, you'll have an enhanced sense of wellbeing. You'll be at your best and people around you will comment, "You're a natural at this." It's like wearing an old pair of comfortable slippers.

"Well great," you say, "but how do you find that fit?" Start by looking at what you're passionate about, care about, or minimally, what interests you. Take it seriously. Ask yourself, "Could I turn this into a business I would love?"

Another way to discover what business may be the right fit for you is to pay attention to your complaints. Do you ever think to yourself or grumble to friends, "I could do a much better job than that?" That's how I began my business. Years ago when I went through my own life transition, I attended a career development workshop. The leader did a great job of imparting information but obviously was uncomfortable interacting with people.

When it was over, she looked relieved. It was no surprise when she didn't offer ongoing support to the participants.

From that workshop I decided to move into the field of Training and Development. Because this was a career change, I experienced first-hand how difficult it was. I felt convinced that many people could use ongoing support in this process and thought I could improve on what the leader had offered. By that time, I had already worked as a social worker, teacher, and therapist, and knew I loved to coach people, nurture their success, and stick with them through thick and thin. I also enjoyed designing workshops, loved leading groups, and could talk endlessly to people about their work. You can see that it was a natural for me to create a business by offering career and professional development coaching.

What about you? Are you driven crazy by how some businesses are run? At a newly opened coffee shop in my neighborhood I walked up to the counter, studied the menu board, and ordered a bagel from the list. "Oh, we don't have any bagels," the girl behind the counter replied indifferently. This is what I mean. I gave it six months. It's gone today. There's definitely room for competition.

Remember Angie and her wish to have a store? She noticed that creating a beautiful and functional in-home office required traveling to many different places, so she came up with the idea to provide everything people needed in one location — paper products, office supplies, desks, chairs, lamps, and laptop carriers. She focused on high quality items that were eco-friendly, beautiful, and unique.

I thought retail could be a great fit for Angie when she confessed she scours flea markets and antique stores and has the ability to spot items that are special, funky, or different. When she shops, she notices things you and I might not. It's in her blood.

On the other hand, you might be motivated by a personal life experience to start a business. Some people decide it's a calling. My client Melanie is convinced we have a serious food problem in our country. She's alarmed about the increase in obesity and diabetes and especially concerned about the food served to children in schools. She's passionate about teaching people to eat healthy food that's produced locally. This is a cause for her that she's turned into a business. She's learned that the food in school lunch programs is mainly heat-and-serve and often loaded with fat, sugar, and salt. In response to this, she's designed a "boot camp" and other programs for food service employees to help them learn how to cook fresh food from scratch. The response so far has been good, but she'll need passion to overcome resistance and habit. It's good this is a cause for her as well as a business.

The key question to ask yourself is: ***What's wanted/ needed/missing that I can offer?*** How can you use your ideas, strengths, and talents to fill that gap? Patricia tuned into her own body to start her business. She noticed how much she needed to stretch and relax after she had been working intensely on the computer for hours. She was sure this was true for coworkers too and started a business providing stress breaks for employees. Already trained as a masseuse, she recruited a cadre of colleagues to give ten-minute massages in the work place. Michael began working as a rigger (hanging lights for events) and then built a multimillion-dollar business leasing equipment and supplying trained riggers because of his passion for excellence and safety. As a pharmacist, Sheila experienced how bad working conditions were for colleagues. She started and grew a nation-wide business placing temporary pharmacists so that permanent employees could have vacations.

A good fit allows you to be authentic and provides a foundation for a vibrant business and a life filled with passion and energy. Thank goodness, there isn't a mold for entrepreneurs. All kinds of people can be successful. Look at business owners you know. Your financial advisor may have earned an MBA and been on a fast track to be a partner in a consulting firm when he went out on his own, while your Yoga teacher who runs a thriving center may have been a housewife who never worked outside her home prior to beginning her business. If you ask successful entrepreneurs how they got started, some will tell you they spent hours writing elaborate business plans. Others jotted notes on napkins. Some began with healthy nest eggs to draw from and others lived paycheck to paycheck before they left their jobs.

Business owners include men and women — young, middle aged, and old. Some are great team players and others are woefully lacking in human relations skills. There are experts and complete novices, extroverts and introverts, people who stumble into starting a business after being fired or downsized, people who plan ahead for years, people who decide to grow a business and hire many employees, and people who prefer to work solo.

There's no mold to fit, but there are four deal-breaking questions related to "fit" that I urge you to answer before you take the leap:

1. Will you be okay working alone (at least initially) or will you miss being part of a company?

A major reason why many people decide not to start a business, or don't stay with it for the long haul, is that they miss being part of the buzz and energy of an existing organization. They want to brainstorm with colleagues and be part of a team. It isn't stimulating enough for them to work alone or with a small group. Solitude feels like isolation. Although many entrepreneurs counter this by taking on a partner, or filling their calendars with coffee dates, participating in joint ventures, and/or becoming active in trade associations or business groups, you may decide that you would be happiest working inside a company.

2. Will you be able to tolerate the insecurity of uncertain income?

Dave decided he could handle it and went out on his own again. But he would tell you in a hot minute that he worried a lot. So far his desire for the freedom to do work he wants to do is greater than his anxiety about money. You'll have to decide if you can sleep at night with financial uncertainty from time to time. As a group, entrepreneurs are extremely optimistic about their abilities to make things happen and many of them figure out that they can reduce worry by socking money away when it's flowing. But that may not be enough to alleviate your concern.

3. Will it be okay (in fact, good) that everything depends on you?

"I'm a great second-in-command," one of my clients asserted, although she could have run any of the companies she was exploring in her job hunt. In the meantime, she easily generated enough consulting projects to keep the bills paid but remained adamant that she wanted to work inside a company in a number two position. Most entrepreneurs love being number one. Do you think you will want to make the decisions, shape the company, and design the future? You better not want it any other way.

4. Will you be able to sell yourself or your products or services?

This last question may be the most important one. Selling yourself is much harder than selling someone else. You don't have to be wildly gregarious, but you do have to find a way to be effective. No sales, no business. Period. The good news is that learning to sell is a skill you can learn, not an inherited gene.

Stephanie had everything she needed to be successful: she was professional, articulate, had great business experience, and had earned an MBA. When she announced she was starting her own business as a consultant to leaders in the health care industry, everyone who knew her was confident she would be successful. She did all the right things: became certified in several training modalities, designed services and programs, crafted speeches, called on executives in companies, and created a website. Audiences raved about her and she was always invited back as a speaker. She also landed a few small contracts, but her savings were dwindling at an alarming rate. "I'm not sure I can make it," she told the members of her support group at one meeting.

We were perplexed and concerned. Yes, the economy was bad, but Dave had started his business around the same time and he was successfully booking work. What was the difference between them? Dave was masterful at selling and extremely confident. He went for big projects and big money. As Stephanie talked, it became clear she had great conversations but lacked the confidence to suggest large projects, ask for the fee she deserved, or go for the close. Fortunately, she's not like one client who confessed, "It's not that I don't like selling myself. It's that I hate it. It's excruciating." Stephanie will succeed because she wants to remain independent, enjoys meeting with people and prospecting for clients and she's determined to master selling.

What about you? I hope you answered these four questions honestly. It's my observation that they're deal-breakers.

If you think you'll be lonely, won't be able to motivate yourself every day unless you're part of a company, and you can't see how to prevent being isolated, don't step out on your own.

If you think you'll worry so much about money you won't be able to sleep at night, don't be an entrepreneur.

If you want someone else to make the decisions, don't start a business.

If you can't promote yourself or ask people to sign on the dotted line and are convinced you'll never learn how to do it, don't even take the first step towards being self-employed.

Well? What do you think? Is being an entrepreneur a good fit?

If your answer is yes, it's time to get into action.

Chapter 5
Don't Scare Yourself to Death

I opened the refrigerator and stared into it, scouting for something to eat. Again. It was only 10:00 AM and I'd already had breakfast.

"I have to *do* something about this," I moaned. My clothing sizes were headed in the wrong direction. And sometimes I didn't get dressed for work all day. "I'm not a real businesswoman. I'm an imposter in pajamas," I thought. Too often I ended up working alone at home. Recently I'd begun to feel lonely. And fat.

By this time, I'd been working for three years in my spare time to build a training and career development business in addition to teaching at a junior college and practicing therapy. I was itching to let go of the teaching and therapy entirely and jump full-time into being a business owner. My salaried friends strongly advised against it, knowing I had no financial reserves. They reminded me that my business was still new and I was operating too close to the wire, but I was passionate. And stubborn. I vowed to take the leap and rent an office downtown, no matter how much it cost. It was that, or become a crazy lady.

I began a search for a location and at the end of 1980 on Christmas Eve day I met a potential landlord. Overextended in his real estate marketing business, he had an empty office to sublet in a suite in the Wrigley Building, an ornate, white high-rise trimmed with shiny copper that sat majestically on the corner of Michigan Avenue and the Chicago River. He showed me a small office that would be perfect. The Wrigley Building. Michigan Avenue. How could I say no? I signed the lease.

Now I had a reason to get dressed, somewhere to go, people around me every day. I felt like a legitimate business owner. A receptionist answered my phone. I had use of a copy machine. At lunch I could walk the Magnificent Mile, a stretch of Michigan Avenue populated with high-end stores, or I could stand on the bridge that spanned the Chicago River and watch boats enter and leave Lake Michigan.

In January 1981 I moved in and months later, expanded by adding a desk in the hallway for a part-time administrative assistant. I thought I was on my way but only two short years later I had to admit that enrollments into my workshops were not keeping up with expenses. The economy was still mired in a deep recession and I had fallen behind on my office rent. In order to survive, I knew I had to quit my business and look for a job, or work from home again. With my ego in tatters, I called my buddy Jake, who ran a successful business and always had great advice.

"I think I have to move back into my apartment. I'm a total failure. I'll never get over this," I sobbed.

"It's just temporary, Robin. You'll move out again soon. I bet it'll only be a year," he said.

Determined to do whatever it took to keep going, I reluctantly moved everything into my one-bedroom apartment in a nearby high rise. Located east of Lake Shore Drive overlooking Lake Michigan, my unit was on the fiftieth floor facing the lake. The building was sixty stories tall, made of shiny black glass, and shaped like ribbon candy. The rent was surprisingly affordable and the building was filled with great energy because many of the 2,000 residents who lived there were entrepreneurs with home-based businesses.

Several years after that move, I stood in my living room and complained to a friend about not being married. She looked around and said, "Robin, there's no room for anyone else here." I looked around. It was true. I'd turned the living room into a workshop space and the cocktail table had disappeared. In the dining area, I'd squeezed my couch between a desk and a copy machine and added another desk for an administrative assistant. There was no dining table. The workshop enrollment board hung in my bedroom. It was the first thing I saw in the morning and the last thing at night.

This conversation was a turning point. I felt ready to take a risk again. I moved my personal belongings into a studio apartment in the same building, kept the first space for my business, and commuted to work by elevator.

Many clients remember attending workshops in this building mesmerized by the breathtaking view. They loved it, yet never knew that much of the time I operated on top of a feeling of failure for having to leave my office on Michigan Avenue. What kept me going was my love for my work and a determination to succeed as an entrepreneur, no matter what. What would I advise you? Take it slow. You don't have to do it like I did. I quit teaching, halted my therapy practice, and began a business and a whole new career at the same time. I never anticipated that the next several years would be terrible economic times. Because I had no savings, I had no safety net. "The wolf" was at my door for many years. While it's true that fear can be a powerful motivator, it can also be paralyzing. There are saner ways to start a business.

Wouldn't it be great to step away from being employed with guaranteed income and work already on the books? If you can, line up contracts and customers before you leave your job. You'll avoid a doubly steep learning curve if you don't change careers at the same time as you start your business. If you're new to a career, work for a while in that area and then start your business after you have some experience behind you.

There are lots of ways to start a business that reduce terror. In 1981, it was the kiss of death to have a home address for a business, but today it's considered smart and environmentally friendly. You can start in your garage, kitchen, or basement and put aside money until you have enough to feel safe renting an outside office. Or, find partners to share the risk. You can build it slowly in your spare time while you're still employed and wait before you leap until the scales are tipped in favor of the business.

Deb is someone who did it right. By the time I met her, she had worked for many years as a Director of Communications in a major corporation. Restless and itchy to do something else, when two senior leaders she liked working closely with left at the same time, she took this as a sign that it was the right time for her to go, too.

"There's something else," she added hesitantly at our first session. "I want to write mysteries." She lamented that after long days at work, she didn't have the time or energy to sit down and write the stories in her mind teasing to be written.

She decided to start a business as a communications consultant and strategist, convinced that would allow her to earn a good income and also give her flexibility and time to work on her personal projects. Before she left her job, she announced her availability for consulting to her best contacts in the company. When she stepped away, she had a great base of business in place already. In her first year her income almost matched her salary and because she worked from home, she had lower expenses.

Since then, because she recognized that it was dangerous to rely on only her former employer for work, she's generated additional clients and begun teaching a course at the university where she earned her Masters Degree. She has also joined a writing support group and is working on a book for young adults.

You don't have to scare yourself to death, but you do have to get started. Don't postpone it by insisting you have to write a detailed business plan first. I know it feels safer to work on a document than get out of your office and ask for business but you can waste weeks on a plan, even months. You might end up trapped in an analysis paralysis and never start your business. If you need a loan to invest in inventory and equipment, you'll probably need a business plan. Otherwise just set aside some time to dream, write goals, and think about how you'll accomplish them. Then get into action. That's all you need because your business will change in ways you can't foresee. You need to be immersed in what you plan to do before you can figure out exactly what business you're in and how best to manage it. Just like technology, most plans end up being outdated within a short time.

It's tempting to think you can't start until you have an office, fancy business cards and stationary, glossy brochures, a sophisticated web site, and an assistant, but if you wait until you have all these in place before you call on potential customers, you're in danger of becoming (or remaining) a closet entrepreneur. These are often the ego trappings we use to hide our insecurities. Of course, there may be a time when it's appropriate to have some or all of these, but in the beginning your job is just to get started.

Yes, I know that prospects usually request something in writing but keep it simple. You certainly don't need a resume because remember, you're not job-hunting. A one-page biographical description is fine. Although a web site is as standard today as having a business card, you can make it simple and embellish it later. It may not be necessary to have an office outside your home or an assistant for a long time, if ever.

Please don't refer to your work as freelancing. If you do, most people will think of it the way the dictionary defines it: "temporary, irregular, or casual." Call your work a business. Think about it as a business. Act like it's a business.

A computer, landline or cell phone, and simple stationary and business cards (maybe only cards) may be all you need to get started. The point is to stop stalling and jump in.

Even if you're new to having a business of your own, you

may already have years of experience with the service or product you're offering. Have confidence in yourself. You don't need elaborate business plans or fancy materials to justify your value.

You can see that there are sane ways to start a business. On the other hand, if you're like me at the time I started, you'll be slightly unbalanced in your passion and not able to wait. If so, you won't pay a single bit of attention to all this very sane advice. You'll probably just leap and then look, like I did.

If you do, I understand totally.

Well, are you ready to make a commitment?

Chapter 6
Put a Stake in the Ground

"I'm not a risk taker," Angie said as she waffled on her idea to open a store. She announced she had turned her attention to getting a job again. What?? Honestly, I didn't know what to say, so I just listened, at least for a while. I understood that justifying a decision not to follow your heart is usually due to fear. I also knew Angie was passionate about her business idea and had two major strengths every entrepreneur needs, the ability to take initiative and to work independently. What I didn't know yet was if her desire for freedom were fierce enough that she would take a risk.

Of course Angie is right that starting a business is risky. Just like getting married, there's no way to know before you actually do it if your business is truly right for you or if it will work. I wish I could promise you'll be successful, but I can't. What I can promise is that waffling will wear you out and drive you crazy, as well as everyone around you. Contrary to what you might think, vacillating creates more anxiety and angst than making a commitment. Everything shifts when you're decisive. You unleash energy, a flow of ideas, and support. People around you respond positively to your commitment and you deepen your belief in yourself.

If you look into your life, you'll discover that every accomplishment you've ever cherished involved some degree of risk. As a teenager, even though you were shy, you may have acted in a play and had a standing ovation. Or in college you ran a successful ice-cream-truck business and made enough money to finance your education. Or as an adult, you ran in a long-distance race and finished it, or took on a mess in a department in your company and turned it into a humming machine, or traveled alone to the Far East, or threw a fabulous party for your parents' fortieth wedding anniversary. Perhaps you took on a fundraising project and raised enough money to make a difference for a cause you believed in, or created a family reunion that people still rave about, or spoke up at a business meeting and although no one agreed with you, ultimately your comments turned the company around. Any accomplishment like this involved enough risk to make your heart race and your palms sweaty. Although difficult, maybe even scary from time to time, on balance it was deeply satisfying and fulfilling, wasn't it?

Starting a business of your own will be that kind of risk. It will change your life forever and is worth doing, no matter what happens. It's the kind of risk that will have you wake up in the morning eager to get started with your day. I'm willing to bet you'll say, "I should have done this a long time ago."

I remember a warm spring day near the end of my senior year in high school. I was sitting in the bleachers with my two close friends, Patti and Judy. We were loyal fans of the boys' track team and attended every meet. That day we were watching Patti's boyfriend practice on the quarter-mile cinder track. As the afternoon sun sank lower in the sky, I became increasingly restless and discontent. I was tired of sitting on the sidelines cheering the boys on, watching them have all the fun. I wanted to run too.

"C'mon, let's go," I shouted as I started down the steps. They shook their heads and looked at me like I was crazy. When I got to the track I ran as far as I could, gasping for breath and laughing my head off. I had to stop several times before I completed the lap. Dressed in saddle shoes, a skirt that came to my calves and a blouse (at that time, the late 1950's, girls didn't wear slacks to school and there was no such thing as a sports bra), I remember being awkward and embarrassed, but far more important, I remember the exhilaration of feeling free.

This small incident is clearly etched in my mind because it's a time when I left the bleachers and got into the game. It was exciting and enlivening. When you jump into your business, it will be the same for you, even if you don't have all the answers. Trust yourself. You'll figure it out.

Yes, you'll be challenged every day. It takes courage, strength, and resilience. There will be times when you'll be afraid, periods when you'll work too hard and your life will be out of balance, and you're certain to make mistakes. From time to time, my successful clients and I have all been scared, worked to the point of exhaustion, and made enough mistakes to qualify as experts.

Leaving a paid job doesn't guarantee a blissful existence. It's like getting a divorce. You'll have the same reaction. Once you're on your own, it's often a shock to discover you still have problems. What's even worse is that you don't have anyone else to blame for them. Your own shortcomings will come into sharp relief. If you're a worrier, you won't stop once you're self-employed. In fact, you may worry more. If you were disorganized or failed to follow up on things when you had a job, it's likely these bad work habits won't disappear. Actually, they may escalate and generate more serious consequences now that you're no longer protected by coworkers or prodded by a boss. Speaking of bosses, you might prove to be a lousy one yourself at first, even if you're the sole employee. Being self-employed is like holding a mirror in front of you and as brilliant as you may be, it's not always pretty.

In order to create something out of nothing and keep it going, you'll have to be bigger than the person you know yourself to be right now. You'll have to dig deep to draw on your inner strength on a daily basis and use every talent and skill you have (and develop new ones). The good news, and the bad news, is that you'll be the only one in charge of your own growth and development. No one else will encourage or pay for it, but no one will stifle it either, and you can work on your shortcomings.

When you're an employee, you learn to follow someone else's lead and wait until you get a green light before you take action. Working in your own business is different. You'll need to take initiative over and over again and make things happen. Even if you grow the business to the point where you have trusted employees, advisors or a board of directors, ultimately the buck stops with you. Knowing all this, are you still willing to take a risk?

Angie finally decided she was. When I asked her what she would do if she could have it any way she wanted, she answered without hesitation, "I'd open a store." Her voice was strong and clear, a clue that this was the truth. She stopped looking for a job. She interviewed storeowners, researched vendors, attended classes, hired a retail consultant, ran numbers, and searched for a location. Finally, she settled on a storefront. She signed the lease and then on the first day, while negotiating with him about build-outs, it became clear that he was backing out of his promises. She walked away.

This was a major breakdown and a real test of her commitment. I held my breath, wondering if she would give up, but she just kept going. She visited new sites and found a better space. Meticulously renovated, the store was attractive, freshly painted, and ready to go. Angie just had to add shelves, stock, and move in. Situated on a corner, it had plenty of windows, good exposure and the exterior was in excellent shape. It was a thousand times better than the place she had almost taken. She proposed a three-year contract and less rent. The landlord agreed to the years but not the rent. Again, I wondered if she would give up.

She didn't. She interviewed owners of other stores on the same street. She returned armed with an impressive business plan and facts on the rental amounts other tenants were currently paying. As she negotiated, Angie's commitment to her business deepened and her self-confidence increased.

The landlord agreed to her terms and in 2009, despite scary newspaper headlines screaming this was the worst economic downturn since the Great Depression, despite Wall Street, insurance companies, banks and the automotive industry begging for bail-outs, despite housing prices in a free-fall and the stock market plunging, despite gloomy predictions for the next one to two years, she put a stake in the ground by signing the lease. She had come a long way since the first day she walked into my office.

At that dark moment when everything fell apart and she had to walk away from the first location, who could have known that she would find another site that was even better? But that's the kind of thing that happens when you make a commitment. When you're at your lowest point, a breakthrough is often just around the corner if you maintain your commitment to your larger vision and keep going. Angie did that by committing to finding a great space, not a specific location.

So what about you? Find some time alone. It doesn't matter where. It could be in your back yard or in a park or busy café, at the library, or in your office with the door closed. Just be sure to turn everything off. Don't answer phones, watch TV, listen to your iPod, talk to anyone, or check emails or text messages.

Get comfortable. Take several deep breaths and allow yourself to let go of all the busyness of your life. Settle into wherever you are. Relax your body and allow your breathing to deepen and become regular. Then, ask yourself: What do I really want? Do I want to be my own boss and have my own business?

Listen to your heart for the answer, not your head. Are you convinced that being self-employed is right for you? Your mind will want to know *how* to do everything before you've even checked in with your heart, so let your heart lead. You'll use your mind plenty later, I promise. What I know is that if your heart's in having your own business, nothing else is going to be right.

If your answer is yes, be your own best cheerleader. Tell yourself (and your mother) that no job is secure today and that you have faith in your own abilities. You'll figure out how to do it – how to make enough money for everything, including perks. You'll find the colleagues and companionship you need. You'll do whatever it takes to make it work.

Your mother's response will hardly matter because at this point you'll be fully committed, but I predict she'll say, "Well, of course, darling. You can do anything you put your mind to."

Okay, now put a stake in the ground that demonstrates to you and the world that you're serious.

Choose a business name.

Set up an office at home, or somewhere else.

Print business cards.

Get a client/customer.

Part II
Adopt Powerful Practices

Chapter 7
Develop Your Muscles

When we met that day for lunch, my friend Kris asked her usual question: "How's your business?"

And I answered optimistically, "It's just around the corner. I can feel it."

"It's just around the corner," she mimicked in a falsetto voice and then added, "I'm sick and tired of hearing you say that. What are you going to do about it?"

Stung, I couldn't answer in the moment. After lunch, I seethed the entire way back to the office and vowed to myself I'd do something to make a dramatic difference by the next time we met.

Kris had started a business placing secretaries in temporary positions the same year I became an entrepreneur. She had ten employees, rented a big office on Michigan Avenue, made tons of money, and dressed like a million bucks. I wanted to be just like her. Despite the fact that she had many years of experience in her industry before going out on her own and also had a partner while I had neither, I fretted about not being at the same level of success as she was. I was passionate and worked long hours, wasn't that enough? Why was I barely making it?

The next time we met for lunch I told Kris I had the solution to my problem — I was going to hire a sales person. After all, successful companies had sales forces, why shouldn't I? She straightened up in her chair, looked me in the eye, and asked, "How in hell are you going to teach someone how to do something you can't do yourself?"

I hated her. I swore all the way back to my office, but I admitted she was right. I dropped the idea and hired an expert to teach me how to sell. Up until then, I'd interpreted every no from a prospective client as a personal rejection and a failure on my part. If I encountered a number of no's in a row, it sent me into a deep funk. Sometimes I was mired in depression for days. After the training, my perspective altered, my mood improved, and I increased enrollments into workshops but not significantly enough to avoid hanging on by a thread that threatened to unravel.

By this time, I had been talking to prospects on the telephone for two years. I spent hour after hour, day after day, with little or no face-to-face interaction. It was a killer. I don't know how I survived as long as I did. Then a colleague suggested I create a face-to-face career review process and it saved my life. I began setting appointments and charging a smaller fee for the review than for a regular coaching session. If people enrolled into a workshop, I applied the fee to it. But whether they did or not, I tried to make the time worthwhile and valuable. This method created a source of small but steady income (a cash cow) and it worked because I was energized and motivated by meeting with people in person. My enrollment percentage improved dramatically.

If there's one skill you must master in order to survive and thrive, it's how to sell. No one will be as enthusiastic or care about your product/service as you do. I'll never forget a past client who attended one of my entrepreneurs' groups for a short time. He had a good business idea but month after month reported he had no clients. Repeatedly, we suggested he get out and talk to people about his service. He refused. His idea, which he considered superior, was to advertise and write articles. Finally he admitted he didn't know how to sell. "Take a sales class," a group member urged. He nodded but never took the step. At every suggestion, he smiled and did nothing. Eventually he dropped out of the group.

Remember Stephanie, my client who was having difficulty landing work? Here's what she did. First, she asked a peer who was good at sales to coach her in how to make calls, what to say and not say. She practiced with her until she felt more confident. Then, understanding that people respond more to the music than the words, she worked on shifting her mental attitude so she could ask for what she was worth.

Like many people, you may hope you can hide in your office and build a business by sending emails but the reality is that at some point you have to meet face-to-face with people to sell your services or products, build trust, and/or open up possibilities. Most of us are at our best in person anyway. We outperform our most fancy materials. One of my entrepreneurial clients worked for months on a sophisticated laptop presentation and after a friend of mine met with her to consider using her services, he told me he was surprised to find she was attractive, lively, and fun — nothing like her formal marketing. He ended up hiring her but it was based solely on who she was as a person.

Even if you had a stellar track record selling a product or service prior to starting your own business, you may find it challenging to sell yourself. It's a much bigger leap than most people anticipate. Many women have the added hurdle of confusing confidence with bragging. They're afraid they'll be accused of being conceited if they promote themselves.

You'll have to learn to take your attention off yourself and put it on the people you're talking to in order to find out what they want and need. Selling is not about you; it's about your customers or clients and how you can help them with the product or service you're offering.

You'll also have to learn that when people say no, it's not personal. In fact, I now know it may not even be final. In some workshops I've led, participants have been present who said no to four previous invitations from me. I've learned that persistence and follow-through make a huge difference.

If you think I was a novice enrolling people into workshops, you should have seen me in my early years trying to land work with companies. It was worse. The only thing that saved me was my enthusiasm and naiveté. Although I was totally inexperienced, it never occurred to me not to go after work inside major companies. At first I didn't have a clue how to describe what I did. To avoid being pigeonholed, I decided to be vague and initially told people I offered, "training in human relations." No one had the foggiest notion what that meant, who to send me to, or how to respond. Their eyes glazed over. They looked at me with polite smiles and murmured, "I see."

If you can describe clearly what you do, you'll give people a handle to help you. It's tempting to sound erudite, use large words, or even worse, industry jargon, but it's a mistake. One of my clients decided he needed a web site as a marketing tool and after completing a first draft, proudly sent the text to me asking for feedback. After reading it I dreaded our conversation, but reminded myself he had asked for honest input and that's what I get paid for. First I complimented him for getting it done and then I delivered the tough love.

"The language is full of corporate jargon. It's complicated, technical, and dry," I said reluctantly. "Make it more personal," I encouraged.

Silence, lasting for an eternity. I wondered if he had hung up.

Finally he said, "I get it. I want my work to be holistic but there's no heart in this, is there?" Exactly.

Plain English works best. The simpler, the better. "I appraise antiques and buy and sell them." "I help company executives craft motivating speeches and communicate clear messages to employees." This is mine: "I help people figure out what they want to be when they grow up, regardless of their age." You get the point.

You can be professional and personable at the same time. I understand if you want to create the impression that you're a company when it's just you, but you're not fooling anyone and the truth is that clients are buying *you*, not just your product or service — and they know it. Just be authentic.

Don't be afraid to let your passion show. Passion is contagious and will pay huge dividends. Even so, you'll have to learn how to close a sale. I remember when I decided to offer a new seminar after a long hiatus from leading workshops. I looked forward to connecting with past clients. After a full day talking to people, I complained to my husband that no one had signed up. "I don't understand it. We had such great conversations," I told him over dinner that night. Then like an ad for V- 8 Juice, I slapped my forehead and said, "Oh, I forgot to ask if they wanted to register."

I had left out those golden closing words: "So, can you do it? Do you want to register? Do the dates and times work?" I know it takes courage to initiate a closing conversation and even today, my stomach knots up a little every time but if you don't do it, you'll be left with all talk and no action.

It's easy to think that if you're good at what you do, that should be enough to grow your business. That's certainly what I thought at first. I just wanted to show up at full workshops and work my magic. I didn't want to have to go after participants. Finally I got the message. You do have to be good at what you do *and* you also have to generate referrals (the lifeblood of any business) *and* you have to close sales so you have clients or customers. If you don't know how to do this yet, just consider it a weak muscle and work on making it stronger.

One last point: if you don't follow through on leads, they're worthless. Spend the time it takes to organize your prospects and note your conversations with each one. If you do that consistently, it will make a huge difference in your results.

No sales? No business. If you learn how to sell your product or service, you won't be sitting in your office sweating with nothing to do, hoping that something will happen, or blaming the world for your lack of success. It's not enough to be passionate; you also need to be skilled. Learning how to sell is a survival tool and your access to thriving. It's worth the investment of your time and energy.

Chapter 8
Connect with Your Tribe

"How's it going?" I asked J.J. We were catching up with each other over coffee at our favorite neighborhood cafe. Okay, so I had a cranberry walnut muffin too.

"I love your suspenders," I told him. They added a quirky note to his colorful retro shirt. His long hair curled around his shirt collar and I thought he looked like the musician he is. Before I met him, J.J. had worked full time in a factory making musical instruments. During that time, he moonlighted by teaching music and performing. After many years, he took a risk and left steady employment to start his own business. At our first meeting, he told me he taught harmonica and drums and performed playing both. I remember thinking, "Oh boy, how in the world is he going to be able to make a living?" But J.J. is an awesome guy and by then he was already successful. He was also ambitious and joined one of my entrepreneurs' support groups for a few years because he wanted to expand his business.

"Last year I had my best year yet," he announced replying to my question. His best year yet? I was impressed, and relieved. We were mired in a deep recession and I'd been afraid his news would be bad, but if there's an audience for J.J.'s skills, he'll find it.

"How do you account for your success?" I asked.

"All those seeds I sowed when I was in your group finally paid off," he said. An exceptional teacher, J.J. loves his students and built his business through referrals, but because he felt nervous about depending solely on the one major referral source he had cultivated, he worked in the group on increasing his contacts. He made proposals to teach classes in numerous public and private schools, created combined parent-child lessons, and experimented with putting together rock groups for teenagers. Today he's teaching in many schools and has tapped into a community of wealthy parents whose incomes have not been greatly affected by the recession. Business is booming because he's found his tribe and mastered selling and marketing.

Large companies have entire departments devoted to marketing and an army of people to implement strategies. As a small business owner, you may be the sole person. You'll have to do everything to help your business survive and grow. So, here's my advice: just do something. Choose an action you enjoy and do it consistently.

If you love to write, then create newsletters, flyers, blogs, postcards or holiday greetings, and send them out regularly. If you thrive on being with people, then attend meetings and conferences or set dates to network over breakfast, lunch, or coffee. If you prefer phone conversations, then make calls. If you keep marketing simple and it's something you enjoy, you're much more likely to do it. Don't get overwhelmed by the myriad of social networking opportunities. Experiment with a few and then stick to what you can handle regularly. It almost doesn't matter what you do, as long as you do *something*.

Putting energy out into the universe comes back in the form of inquiries, referrals, or new prospects. Mysteriously, results don't always track directly with your efforts. Instead, they seem to come out of the blue. It may be a matter of "stirring up the gold dust," as Catherine Ponder called it, the author of many books on prosperity. If you stay in action, ultimately you'll generate new business.

In the meantime, search for your audience. You can't serve everyone. Stephanie began to increase her results when she realized that if she tried to sell to people she didn't connect with, it would be an uphill battle. Because she's African-American and worked for many years inside large organizations prior to starting her business, she understood the challenges minority members confront as they move into leadership positions. The more attention she put on this population, the more passionate she became about it. She began targeting minorities in Health Care, an industry where she had a lot of knowledge and experience, and she found her tribe. As Seth Godin suggests in his book *Tribes*, she is becoming a leader by helping members connect and communicate with each other and by supplying information, wisdom, and support. She's building a presence and reputation with minorities, is booking work, and feeling appreciated. She's on her way.

The only thing that never works is paralysis. When you do something and it works, you create an upward spiral of energy. You're motivated to keep going and do more. Yes, some marketing methods are more effective than others. You have to discover what works best for you and your business. I remember at a volunteer event, a friend turned to me and said, "I used to come to this to promote my business but I don't any more." When I asked her why, she said, "It proved to be a waste of my time." You'll need to be discerning, but be sure to try an activity you enjoy a couple of times before you decide it won't work.

Here's the bottom line, the most brilliant marketing plans are useless if you can't, or won't, do them. Take on learning how to market with the same intensity as learning how to sell. Read books and/or follow consultants online like Robert Middleton, a marketing guru who will help you grow your business.

A warning: don't hire marketing consultants who don't understand what it's like to do everything yourself, or to have a small staff and a small budget. Otherwise, your fee will go down the drain, along with all their elaborate, unrealistic plans.

I know it can be hard to keep going when you're waiting for results but marketing is a lot like tending a garden. You sow seeds and for a while, it looks like nothing is happening. That's the time when you need to have faith that your efforts will ultimately produce results. Don't get discouraged and give up too soon.

My friend Cathy told me about a colleague who called her about the possibility of subcontract work. Because Cathy had been working successfully as a consultant for ten years, she understood how scared and desperate her colleague felt. Although she didn't have any work for her at the time, Cathy encouraged her to hold on. A month or two later, Cathy contacted her about work she had just landed "that would have kept her busy for months" and discovered she had already taken a job. Too bad.

A business advisor I had for years used to encourage me to sow seeds by having at least ten to twelve proposals out to companies at any one time. He claimed three companies would say yes almost as soon as I walked in the door, no matter what I did; three would say no, regardless of what I did; and the other four would need to be nurtured with the hope that at least one of them might convert to a client at some point. In a tough economy, these numbers are probably higher, but having a number out in front of you to target each month is a great way to manage yourself. Once I got started, I usually never had to set as many appointments as I initially thought because I got busy pretty quickly.

Your purpose for marketing is to create a presence in the market place, introduce your business to potential new clients, lay the groundwork for the future, and open the door for selling. It's also to remind past customers and clients that you're still in business. Because a high percentage of businesses fail or people decide self-employment is not right for them, you need to let everyone know you're still in the game. I'm amazed at the number of people who ask if I'm still coaching people. It's easy to assume everyone knows but they don't.

Even after thirty years, my stomach churns when I have a small amount of business projected on the books. From past experience, I know I can count on some money coming in throughout the year but often I don't have any idea how I'll make up the rest. Whenever I look at a blank calendar, my heart beats faster. It took a long time before I learned how to manage myself. Now I know I have to be careful not to feed my anxiety.

If I start to spiral into panic, I literally tell myself "Stop!" and shift my attention to what I want to create in the future. I list all the steps I know that will generate business. That usually calms me down right away. Then I get busy taking them, one at a time, trusting to the future. Although I may not produce results immediately, I know the more energy I put out, the more will come back to me at some point in the form of opportunities.

If you market consistently, I predict you'll create work. All small businesses experience periods with little or no work followed by periods with lots of work. It's a desert or rain forest cycle. Don't worry. Learn to save money when business is going well and you'll have it when you need it. Then when it's quiet, get into action and market, market, market. Sell, sell, sell. If you do, I promise it will soon be work, work, work again. Before you know it, you'll wish you had more free time.

Now that you know what the two most important skills are, you're all set, right?

Well, no.

Hold on. It can be a wild ride.

81

Chapter 9
Navigate Bumpy Roads and Potholes

Before I even made the presentation, I was hooked. I was dying to win a training contract with the bank. This wasn't just any bank. It was exceptional — successful, progressive, and with a national reputation for investing in the surrounding community. These were my kind of values. The meeting went well and they requested a proposal. I spent hours crafting it, then mailed it, and waited. Then I called. And called and called.

It isn't that they never returned my calls; it's just that sometimes it took weeks. Each time they encouraged me and told me to call again. I became a victim of hope because they never said no. Eventually they wore me out. Weeks turned into months before I accepted the fact that it was never going to happen.

In the meantime, I'd wasted time and energy and something

else very dangerous had happened. Secretly I'd begun to count on the work coming through and had slowed down my efforts to generate other possibilities. I pictured myself leading trainings in the company and even dreamed about what I'd do with the money. I almost spent it. One time, in a different situation, I did that.

On a late Friday afternoon, I talked to a prospective client. Excited about what I proposed for his company, he said, "Okay, let's do it." On Saturday I went shopping and bought clothes for work, convinced I needed them. I spent almost the entire amount of the contract. On Monday he called to say he couldn't do it after all. Ouch.

Adding to my list of mistakes, my first year in business I hired a graphic artist to design brochures advertising a series of public workshops I planned to offer. She did a great job and when they were done, I was thrilled. The cost was a fortune to me at the time but I ordered seven hundred and took them to a convention where I shared a table with another entrepreneur. For three days we worked long hours, standing on our feet from early morning until evening. It was my first experience at a trade show and I assumed people would flock to our table and sign up on the spot. I was confident I would fill my workshops.

To my surprise, I discovered I was shy with strangers and had to push myself to make contact with the streams of people who walked by largely ignoring me. Although I managed to reach many people over the three days, only a few of the thousands who passed by actually stopped to talk or ask questions and no one signed up for a workshop. Of course I was disappointed but I was still optimistic that enrollments would roll in over the next couple of weeks.

Back home, I soaked my sore feet and waited for the phone to ring and registrations to arrive in the mail. I waited. And waited.

Zilch.

Nada.

The dates for the workshops came and went. No one enrolled. No one even claimed the one free spot I had offered in a drawing. Devastated, I stared in despair at an empty calendar, a measly bank account, a box filled with hundreds of useless, outdated brochures, and a defunct business plan based on projected workshop attendance.

I've had to learn about proposals too. I discovered that salaried employees have a different experience of time than we do as entrepreneurs. They're happy to talk and talk and talk in an appointment and then encourage you to write detailed proposals. But for you and me, time *is* money and we have to protect it. In the past I wasted a lot of time on proposals that went nowhere. Today I don't even write one unless I'm 90% sure I have the contract and I keep it as short as possible. It's not worth more effort unless the project is complex, has huge potential, and you have a strong chance to win it.

Trust me, until you've been doing it for a while, you won't know exactly what your business will be, how best to market and sell your services or products, who your customers really are, and what you'll end up offering successfully. Along the way, you'll figure out which doors open easily and which are unyielding, what modifications or changes you need to make in what you offer, and even what you do and don't enjoy in your work. There will be a lot to learn and some surprises, so stay open to change.

"I didn't know it would be like this," Angie complained at a monthly entrepreneurs' meeting. "What do you mean?" we asked.

"I'm alone a lot and miss colleagues. I even miss the graphic design work I used to do. I don't feel creative," she said. When we reminded her of how extraordinarily creative she had been in setting up her store, she said, "That's done. It's not enough now."

Months ago, we had suggested she offer design services in addition to selling products to increase income. She hadn't been ready to do it then, but now she agreed that the time might be right. Soon after that meeting a customer came into her store to buy items for his office. He also asked if she knew someone to help with a design for a logo, business cards, and stationary. It was right up her alley. The extra work added a creative spark and also helped pay the rent. In the process she created a second profit center that fit right in with her primary business. Angie was surprised to discover that she needed more creative outlets than the store to feel happy at work. Her awareness illustrates that you can't know how your business will work best for you until you actually do it.

Although I'm glad to share my hard-learned lessons with you, there's no way I can protect you from the mistakes you'll make. Here's the good thing about failures. You can learn from them and then put good practices in place so you don't repeat them. From the mistakes I shared above, I've learned: don't get too attached to one potential piece of business; don't invest in expensive market-ing until you know what your business is (maybe never); be careful about printing dates on materials; don't spend the money until the check is in the bank (and cleared); and don't spend time writing elaborate proposals when one page will do it.

I've also learned about the danger of overly depending on one client to survive. Early in the life of my business, my pal Sid encouraged me to participate in a volunteer project. I declined because I told him I didn't have the time and needed to keep my attention on my business. Sid was enthusiastic and persuasive, so eventually I gave in. "It will come back tenfold," he promised. The group of volunteers included entrepreneurs and corporate repre-sentatives who were exploring how to help make a difference in the Chicago public schools. After several meetings, a woman from Human Resources at a major company approached me, comment-ed that she liked how I interacted with people, and asked, "Will you meet with me to discuss a project we're considering inside the company?" That meeting led to three years of work co-designing and co-leading trainings for employees. It was an engrossing project and demanded a lot of my time and energy. The revenue from it comprised a large portion of total company income and helped pay office rent and salaries.

The whole time I was engaged in this project, warning bells kept going off in my head: "This is going to end some day. It's dangerous to depend so much on one client. You should be marketing to other companies." But, I found myself constitutionally incapable of leading those trainings and marketing at the same time. It began to feel like I was riding a train headed towards a cliff and couldn't do anything about it except hope the landing wouldn't be too bad.

In the third year of the project, still convinced I had plenty of time, I hadn't done anything yet about generating new clients. Then with no warning, my colleague at the company announced they were pulling the plug on our work in ten days. And that was that. I was confronted with a blank calendar and a huge revenue hole. It was a major setback. I was gripped by fear for a while but then I got back up on my feet again and created new services to fill the gap.

It's absolutely best if you can provide a service and look for new work at the same time. But if you can't, then just focus on doing great work with your client, sock money away, and get back to marketing when you're not busy. There's one exception to this

— if your whole business depends on only one client, that's way too dangerous. Even for me.

One of my favorite cartoons is a picture of a man standing in front of a flip chart with a graph of a bell curve. The curve goes straight up, like a mountain, and then heads sharply straight down. Way down. He's pointing at the top of the "mountain" and the caption underneath reads, "And then something happened...."

If you have a small business, even in the best of times, something dicey can happen: a major contractor cancels a project; a close family member gets sick or dies; you become ill and are knocked out of the box for a while; a sleazy customer doesn't pay; you vastly underestimate the cost and time for a project; checks bounce; people don't answer phone calls or e-mails; a company keeps you on the hook for months for an answer to your proposal (and then says no); companies don't pay when they say they will (the bigger they are, the worse they tend to be); the building where you have your business converts to condominiums and you have to move; your local government decides to re-pave the street in front of your business, the road is blocked by construction vehicles and there's nowhere for customers to park; a marketing program doesn't generate the results you anticipated; an employee embezzles money or steals products; you lose a key contact at a company because they leave, are promoted, transferred, or fired, and you have to start all over again; someone terrific you hired and trained moves, has a baby and decides to stay home, goes to work for a competitor, or starts a competing business.

You can count on some or all of these events occurring in the lifetime of your business. If you think about your own experience working for companies, you know every business has its ups and downs. We just never think the down times will happen to us. If you're a one‑person show, or have a small staff and operate close to the wire, you'll be impacted much more dramatically than large companies with deep pockets and lots of employees. For them, these events are blips on a screen. For us, they're a matter of survival. Most of them are beyond our control. The best thing you can do is to focus on managing your response to what happens.

It would be easy to panic or become paralyzed by fear, cut corners to save money, ignore your intuition, take the easy way out, get mired in depression, succumb to negativity, become rigid or isolated, settle for less than you're proud of, become disengaged, lose touch with your passion, or become resigned. But if *you're* in trouble, the business is in trouble. If you get stopped, or if you refuse to listen to good advice, the business suffers. When times are tough, focus on managing yourself. Dig deep to find your strength. Draw on your resilience, ask for help, get into action, hold true to your convictions, trust your intuition, stick with it, refuse to settle, and surround yourself with positive input.

Colin is someone who knows all about ups and downs. He

began his business twenty years ago by cleaning out the homes of people who died and then selling the valuable items he found. He became an expert on "stuff" at the same time that it appeared that he also became a victim of it.

His health took a nosedive and he was often ill with bad colds, aching, and no energy. He had to take days off from work. Thinking it was an allergy to dust and molds in the basements and attics where most of his work took place, he hired people to help and gradually shifted his focus to appraising and buying. Even this change didn't end the bouts of illness. Finally after many years of dogged research to figure out what was wrong, Colin was diagnosed with Chronic Fatigue Syndrome.

He changed his business dramatically and stopped clean-outs entirely. Now he only buys and sells high-end antiques online and in a brick and mortar showroom that he humorously describes as "the world's most difficult retail space to find." Tucked away in an alley, his store is only open limited hours because insomnia is one of the debilitating symptoms he experiences with flare-ups and he might need to sleep late into the morning.

He takes good care of himself, eats well, manages his energy, and over the years, his health has improved but sometimes he has discouraging setbacks. Fortunately, he refuses to become resigned and continues to work at managing his attitude. Because he's self-employed, he can be flexible and design his business to accommodate his condition. None of this was predictable when Colin started his business many years ago.

There are lots of challenges to meet as entrepreneurs but one of the hardest is when business slows down. It happens no matter how successful you are and can stir up fear and anxiety. Having money in the bank helps but it's also good to learn to appreciate slow times as a gift. They're ideal for fostering creativity and inventiveness because when you're busy it's hard to carve out time to dream. Looking back, I see these were the times when I came up with a new product or service. Some of my clients use slow periods to catch up. Sue cleans her desk and files, updates bookkeeping, straightens up the office, and puts procedures in place. This is calming work for her and she feels like she is laying the foundation for a busy future. Mary rests and sometimes takes a vacation. Other entrepreneurs spend time planning, decide to work fewer hours, or hang out with their families.

As a small business owner, you'll experience highs you can't imagine. But even if you're talented, passionate, and work hard, you'll also confront failures, disappointments, and slow times. In short, the whole human experience.

By now, it's probably clear that the real bottom line is to master the art of managing yourself.

Chapter 10
Take the Squeaky Chair Test

"I think I'll start writing business plans and corporate annual reports," Nan announced.

As a newly independent writer, my client had been struggling to land contracts in the health care arena. Now she was trying to convince me she could market herself in two different directions at the same time.

"Are you even interested in business?" I asked.

"Well, no," she answered, "but I could make good money."

"Hmmm. Where did this idea come from?" I asked. She admitted that a successful business writer (namely, her husband) had suggested it.

Later in that same session I discovered that she was deeply discouraged because just a few days ago she had experienced a big setback; a writing assignment she had counted on had fallen through. No wonder she was feeling uncertain and ready to give up. With twenty years of experience writing on health care issues she wasn't a novice, but she was still a beginner at being self-employed. She needed to learn how to market and sell her services.

"What do you think would happen if you took that energy you're putting into trying to break into business writing and put it back into generating assignments in the area that really interests you?" I asked.

It was clear to me that if she followed the well-intentioned advice of her husband, and tried to sell her services in two areas at the same time, it would keep her in a swirl and undermine her results. Instead, I advised her to honor what interested her, focus on one area, renew her commitment to that, and redouble efforts in that arena.

Building a business is a lot like planting a tree. First you need to put down deep roots and grow a strong trunk by focusing on one thing. Later, you can branch out in different directions and create new profit centers. Just don't do it before you've built a solid core.

I've seen many small stores in the area where I live fail because they make the mistake of going in too many directions at once. The pattern is always the same. Without enthusiastic customers filling the shop, the owner becomes frantic and throws in anything she can think of to survive. First, she starts her store as a bakery and sells cookies, muffins, and cakes. The problem is that they're nothing to holler about and business is really slow. A short while later, she adds soup and sandwiches and you begin to wonder if maybe it's a restaurant. Then, before you know it, she's selling stuffed rabbits, the kiss of death. "What business is she in anyway?" you wonder.

Staying committed is the work of your first year in business — committed to being self-employed and committed to one direction. Being committed is different from trying, hoping, wishing, or wanting. It means giving 100%, and it's not easy. Some businesses take off right away. I hope your business does, but for many people, it's slow growth for a while. In the beginning, it often requires nine units of energy out, with only one returned in the form of results. It can take years to create the momentum to reverse these numbers.

No wonder the early years are a time when it's easy to panic and get sidetracked. You might even be tempted to look for a job at the same time you're trying to get your business off the ground. Some of my clients have thought this would be a smart idea, assuring me they needed an "ace in the hole." I strongly discourage it. The truth is that looking for a job is a diversion from the hard work required to get a business up and running.

I know about this because I took a number of detours early

in my business. I remember one time when I felt ready to give up. I decided to apply for a job that sounded mildly interesting (yawn) in the marketing department of a hospital. I got an appointment and put on my best business clothes to sell myself in the interview.

As I walked down the halls, my heels clicked on the shiny floors. The gleaming white walls felt cold and sterile, nothing like my cozy home office overlooking the lake. I shivered. Then someone much younger who didn't have the education or experience I did and clearly didn't know what he was doing, interviewed me. I sighed. The possibility of having someone like him as my boss was the very reason I had started my business in the first place.

I took charge of the conversation to help it along but as the hour progressed, my spirits sank. I slumped in the chair and found it hard to breathe. By the time it ended, I bolted into the sunshine, took a deep breath and felt so relieved to be self-employed that I decided anything I had to face in my own business was better than working for someone else. Hal Wright, my business advisor, would have said my chair had squeaked.

Hal introduced me to the squeaky chair phenomenon. Whenever he met with new business owners in his home office, he sat them in a rocking chair in the living room. If they leaned forward and began the meeting by whining and complaining about their business, and continued despite Hal's reassurances, he would say, "Well, you can always quit and get a job." Then if they leaned back, the chair squeaked, and they replied, "Well, now, just a minute," he knew they were not ready to call it quits. So after I heard my own "chair squeak" in that job interview, I redoubled my efforts to make my business work.

I confess that not only did I pursue that hospital job, but in my second year of business I also accepted a job offer on a Friday, changed my mind over the weekend, and resigned on Monday. And in dark times in the early years, I allowed myself to be seduced by more than one multi-level marketing firm. Steeped in magical thinking, I convinced myself that I could build that business part-time (don't even ask me which one) while I still kept growing my own business.

"You'd be good at it. You already know how to sell and you have a big network," the recruiters always said. They also claimed they made more money than I did with much less effort. Because anything looked easier than what I was trying to do at the time, I'd start enthusiastically. I'd have some initial success and think, "This is great. This is easy." Then I'd inevitably reach the point where I had run through my hot leads and suddenly it became hard. I'd realize I was up against the very same challenges I was confronting in growing my own business.

"What in the world am I doing?" I'd wonder. Ultimately I'd quit and with a red face, return to my business. I think sometimes friends didn't know whether I was a career coach or a vitamin sales rep. The good thing about those forays was that I always returned to my business more determined than ever to make it work. They forced me to answer the question: If I could make my business work, would I rather stick with that? The answer was always yes.

No business is easy. Period. No matter what people tell you. If it looks and sounds too easy and not everyone is doing it, be suspicious. It's not what it looks like. If you have a business, the truth is you'll have to work hard and stick with it to succeed. Decide to be single-minded, laser-focused, and consistent. Don't waffle or allow yourself to get sidetracked by diversions.

Although making a commitment is the major challenge of your first year, you'll discover it's not a one-time event. Commitment will come up as an issue multiple times in the life of your business. You'll go through slumps. You'll get tired or bored. At times, you'll feel overwhelmed. Every entrepreneur does. The good news is these challenges allow you to choose all over again.

This is the time to remind yourself why you became an entrepreneur in the first place, to rekindle your vision, tap into desire, and deepen your commitment.

You'll be inspired all over again.

Chapter 11
Get a Grip — Money, Money, Money

"WHAT? HOW IN THE WORLD COULD I OWE THAT MUCH?" I yelled as Ruth sat next to me on the couch, hands folded in her lap, waiting quietly until I calmed down. "How could the IRS and I look at the same numbers in such different ways?" I wailed to my accountant.

There's a lot to learn about money when you have a business. The spring of my first year as an entrepreneur I was dating a CPA. When taxes were due, he offered to file my return for free. He determined the amount I owed was small because I made so little money that year and had lived mainly on credit cards. The following April we weren't dating any more and when I called to find out what I should do, he asked, "Did you make the same as last year?" I looked at my tiny checking account balance and answered yes. Without seeing any numbers, he casually advised, "Don't worry then." The IRS disagreed.

Was it revenge for a failed relationship, or just bad advice? I'll never know. It literally took me years to dig out from under. Now I owed the Government, had credit card debt, and was behind with vendors. Taxes were the worst. Getting on top of them was like climbing a slippery slope — until back taxes were paid, interest and penalties kept accumulating, and then before I knew it, current estimated taxes were due... and at the same time new business expenses cropped up and...

From a small hill, my debt grew into a mountain. It was an albatross, sapping my energy and enthusiasm. I had to do something or it would sink me. Finally I decided to hire an accountant, not date one. I sat in his large, well-appointed office and humbly laid out all the bad news. I hoped he'd have a magic solution. I admitted that I'd been waiting for the "big one," a contract large enough that I could pay all the bills at once, but now I suspected there was no such thing. He confirmed my doubts, adding that most people continue to cling to the fantasy of a miracle business deal and end up digging an even deeper hole. I felt reassured by his comment, even a little hopeful, but then he delivered a stunning blow. He advised I declare bankruptcy, cut my losses, and shut down the business.

This may have been one of the lowest points in my life. It

may also have been the moment I knew for sure I would keep going. He saw numbers on a page. What he didn't see was how stubborn and passionate I was to make my business work. I left his office and after several humiliating and stressful conversations with the IRS, worked out an agreement to pay what I owed in installments. Then I made a list of everyone I owed money to, set up a payment plan, and talked to each person about it. Little by little, month after month, year after year, I paid off the debts. I also hired Ruth as my accountant and we've worked together ever since to make sure I never get into that kind of trouble again, especially with taxes.

Many people start businesses because they love the service or product they're offering and they're drawn to the idea of having something of their own, but that doesn't mean they understand how to handle finances. I remember two young men who came to see me for advice. They had been partners for three years and had a busy landscaping business.

"What are you concerned about?" I asked.

"We don't know if we're making money or if we're in trouble," one of them responded.

"What does your accountant say?" I asked.

"He never answers our questions," he complained. These were smart, capable men. I suggested they assert themselves and demand an answer, or find a new accountant. "You need to get involved in the numbers," I told them.

It's tricky though. For many years I obsessed about the numbers and I can tell you, that doesn't work. It's important to have a budget and review it often, but I know from experience that too much attention on money (and worry) is debilitating. It distracts you from what you need to focus on — accomplishing your goal. But be sure you don't have your head in the sand either. Delegating is one thing. Dumping is another. You will need to find a balance. It's best to use numbers as a fix on reality and a source of motivation.

Your business mantra should be: more money in than out. It's simple, but not easy. There are only two ways to do that: increase revenues and/or cut expenses. You have to figure out how much money it takes to run your business and provide a living, and then generate enough to cover both. A graphic designer I know who has had her own business for twenty years reminded me how important it is to charge high enough fees.

"These young designers who are charging $15.00 an hour don't get it," she said. "Not only can they not support themselves on that, they're undermining the whole industry. They should charge two to three times that, or more." Optimistically you may think that all your hours of work will be billable or filled with selling, but that doesn't take into account all the time needed to set up meetings, make presentations, tend the books, do marketing, etc. That time has to be paid too. And even if you don't have employees, you will probably need the services of an accountant and/or a lawyer. You have to charge enough to meet business and personal expenses and build in extra (it's called profit) so that you can reward yourself and your employees, keep the business afloat in tough times, and invest in growth, if that's your goal.

If you're not mindful, you can easily end up starving your business to feed your ego. Inevitably new people you meet in the course of doing business ask: where's your office and how many employees do you have? It's tempting to take on a fancy office, many employees, slick materials, and a new car. However, they don't make a business great. *You* do. Just focus on what you need in order to do excellent work.

If you compare yourself to other business owners, someone will always do better than you and no amount you earn will ever be enough. I've had clients who made more money in one deal than I have in ten years. The money you can earn depends largely on what you offer and who your audience is. It doesn't mean one person or service is more valuable than the other and you may decide that making a lot of money demands too much from you. It's not worth what it takes to earn it. Jen said that recently. Last year in her business as a communications consultant, she earned a huge amount of money but she paid a high price for it. She had months of unending, boring, and stressful work with clients she didn't like. She announced she'd never do that again. I suggested she think about how to earn that much doing work she really enjoys, with clients she likes but if she can't see a way to do that, I know she'll be happy with less as long as she's doing the work she loves.

Having a full, rounded life may be more important to you than making more income. It is to me. Instead of working all the time, you may want time to travel, hang out with friends and family, or attend classes or workshops. Successful business owner and author, Paul Hawkens urges, "Always leave enough time in your life to do something that makes you happy, satisfied, even joyous. That has more of an effect on economic well-being than any other single factor."

Maybe you know a lot about managing money already but I'm aware that many smart, successful people are financially ignorant. Even wealthy people may know very little about money. So here are a few things I've learned from my clients and my own experience. Credit card debt is costly and because it represents the past, it's dead energy. You probably don't even remember what you spent the money for in the first place. Pay it off as quickly as you can and don't use the cards again unless you can pay them in full monthly or have no other alternative. Owing money causes most people a lot of anxiety and is energy draining so think carefully about how much debt you can handle.

It's always best to manage your business with a high level of integrity right from the start. If you do have debt, the most important thing is to set payments low enough so that you can pay consistently and keep your word. If you get behind, restore your integrity immediately by getting into communication. Being debt free is a great goal to have. It's what most of us want. It's a part of that freedom we love.

Even if you work alone, hire an accountant. I appreciate Ruth because she's a straight arrow and that works for me. We've put systems in place to make sure I do the right things at the right time so there are no surprises. A good accountant helps you follow rules and regulations, set aside money for taxes or payroll, and prevent mistakes with paperwork that can have costly penalties. Then your attention and energy can be freed up to work on making your business successful. Just be sure your accountant is someone who understands you, your business, and the human side of your work as well as the numbers.

Two last pieces of advice: Don't mess with the IRS. Period. And don't date your accountant.

Chapter 12
Find a Solid Footing

I was holding on by my fingernails, and they were a mess. Still new to my business, I was desperately trying to figure out how to generate more money flowing in than out. When a friend suggested I meet with a successful businessman she knew who might be able to help, I jumped at the chance. Secretly I hoped he might rescue me.

He agreed to see me in his office. I was in my early forties then and quite "hot" if I do say so — single, sexy, and available. I wore my favorite tight-fitting lavender suit with a slit up the back and three-inch heels. After talking briefly, he suggested we continue over dinner. I figured he preferred evening because he was too busy with work during the day. After all, he was doing a favor to meet with me in the first place.

He was middle-aged, a little pudgy, a little balding, and a little vague about his exact business. At dinner that night I became increasingly frustrated because he was not giving me ideas how to improve my business. Finally he offered to set me up. Well, that sounded more hopeful. Did he mean provide financial help? Yes, he answered and then described the place he would choose for me to live.

Wait a minute. I already had an apartment. When he said he would buy the right clothes for me to wear, I finally got it. The lights came on. He wanted me to be a kept woman, *his* kept woman. Regardless of how scared I was about my uncertain future, I was insulted. How dare he think he could pick out my clothes!

Seriously, I was angry. He missed the whole point. In that moment I knew I didn't really want to be rescued. I just wanted to learn how to run my business successfully so I could stand on my own two feet. I needed help, not a sugar daddy.

I learned that night that a rescue could be more disempowering than empowering. It's never free. You can be sure the price will be high, much too high. It's a better use of your time to dig deep to discover your strengths than look for someone to save you. What you really need is to learn how to make your business work. However, occasionally you might also need the help of an angel.

That same difficult year I often headed to a private exercise club to work out and take my mind off worries. Although it was expensive, I didn't consider it a luxury and decided not to drop my membership because I was convinced that I'd eventually land business through contacts I made there.

One day I stopped to chat with a friend as he was leaving the club. We had met on the indoor track. As we ran together, we talked about work, taking our minds off our aching bodies and the tedium of running laps. He was an entrepreneur who had started his business from home mixing glue in his garage. By the time I met him, he was so successful making adhesives that he owned an entire building. He was interesting and encouraging.

"How's it going?" he asked. I laughed and deliberately kept my voice light as I replied, "Great, except I don't know how I'm going to buy groceries." I don't know how he recognized the real fear underneath my laughter or why he didn't question how I could be going to an expensive club but couldn't put food on the table. At the end of our conversation, he reached in his pocket and gave me $100.00. There were never any strings attached. Later when I attempted to pay him back, he tore up the check and sent it back to me. That money made a huge difference to me. It not only paid for food, it also represented the psychic lifeline I needed to keep going. He was my first angel.

I met my second angel in a bank. I desperately needed a loan to continue building my business, but had already been turned down by two local banks. It was a time when most men, and many females, doubted women could be successful business owners. When a colleague suggested I talk to a female loan officer she knew at a large downtown bank, I wondered if it would be worth it but decided to follow up on her suggestion. I arrived with flyers describing workshops I wanted to offer, admitted I had no collateral or savings and told her I was pouring whatever money I made right back into the business. She listened carefully. "Here's how we'll do it," she whispered as she drew up the request in the form of a personal loan. "We won't tell them it's for your business." The loan was approved and I never missed a payment. I think about her often with deep gratitude.

And then there was my mother.

As a new entrepreneur, nothing had prepared me for a recession. One after the other, training contracts evaporated that I had counted on, even with well-established companies. I had no back-up plan, no experience with generating income quickly, and no financial cushion. Desperate, I decided I to sell my car to pay the rent.

Even though I didn't have to drive often because I lived downtown in an apartment within walking distance of public transportation and stores, the decision was wrenching. My car had been a symbol of independence and freedom since my early twenties. Still, I was determined to do whatever it took to remain self-employed.

On the day I sold my car I had a blind date for dinner. I hardly noticed the restaurant we went to and just moved food around on my plate. As I talked about what I had done, I started to cry. Okay, I admit I wasn't much fun, but my date wasn't even close to meeting angel criteria in the empathy arena. He brought me home early. That night I cried myself to sleep. Early the next morning, the telephone woke me up.

"What's wrong, Robin?" my mother asked. "I had the feeling I should call you."

I was amazed. I had talked to her just three days earlier as part of our weekly phone ritual. I'd been careful not to reveal how worried I was and had never mentioned that I had to sell the car. It was unusual for us to talk again so soon. Now caught in a vulnerable early-morning state of half awake and half asleep, I couldn't hide my grief and fear. "I sold my car to pay the rent. I'm afraid I'm not going to make it," I blurted.

Several weeks earlier my mother had visited me and sat in the back of the room, watching as I led a workshop. She was adamant that I not give up. "People need this," she declared firmly. She told me to sit down, figure out how much money I needed to curb my panic, and then call her back.

This turned out to be one of the best exercises I've ever done. The words "curb your panic" were the key. She didn't suggest that I come up with the amount of money I needed to clear up my entire debt, or to hire people, or to launch a marketing campaign. Just the amount I needed to calm down. That was a powerful exercise.

It's good to write numbers down on paper in black and white, especially when you feel scared or overwhelmed. Situations quickly escalate into catastrophes in your imagination but are rarely as dire as you imagine. Even if they are as bad or even worse than you thought, putting them down on paper will grant you distance and perspective.

I did what my mother suggested and called her back the next day. She loaned me the amount of money I needed and wisely threw in a little extra knowing that would give me more breathing room.

Years later when we talked about that day, I told her, "You were like a mother lion protecting her cub." "I was, wasn't I?" she said, sounding pleased. Her fierce belief in me, along with the loan, allowed me to calm down and come up with ideas on how to generate income.

This is how I handled the loan with my mother. It's what I also advise you to do with loans from family or friends. I set up a payment plan, wrote up an agreement and sent it to her even though she assured me I didn't need to do that. I insisted though because I knew it would ensure having an adult relationship with her and as long as I kept my word and paid her back on time, I

would feel free to be open about doing things for myself occasionally, like taking a vacation.

Now if my clients talk rapidly, hyperventilate, and try to
convince me they need to give up, I tell them, "The first thing
you need to do is calm down." As my mother suggested, curb your
panic. Everything looks different when you slow down and take
deep breaths. You can figure out what you need and what to do
about it. Then, get to work.

You never know where help will come from, or in what form.
Sometimes all you need is encouragement, inspiration, a good
idea, or a lucky break. One thing is for sure: you don't need to be
rescued. You'll never learn anything from that. But a loan with
clear parameters, a line of credit, or a small gift of money from an
angel can help you get over a tough hurdle in the short term and
give you the confidence to keep going.

Dealing with money is a rich source of spiritual lessons if we
recognize them. Over and over again, my lessons have had to do
with trust. My father died when I was eighteen and every time I
confront financial uncertainty I revert emotionally to that scared
teenager. Reality and my previous track record have no impact on
this fear. While trying to be reassuring at such times, friends have
often said, "You've always been taken care of, you always will be."
When I think of all the people in the world who need to be taken
care of and aren't, this never works for me. But recently a friend

said, "You'll figure it out. You always do." That felt right. I can trust myself to figure it out — and trust my higher power to guide me. In hard times, this thought may comfort you too.

I don't know what your spiritual lesson will be. Maybe it will have to do with compassion, or generosity, or integrity. It will be there. Just look for it.

If there's one area in your life you need to learn about, develop mastery in, and bring maturity, wisdom, and integrity to, it's money.

It's the hard work we all need to do.

Chapter 13
Ride Slow Trains

I opened the curtains in our tiny bedroom as the train wound around a curve. It was early morning and we were in Colorado. Yesterday, late in the afternoon, we had departed from Chicago. We had left behind winding rivers, flat grasslands, and small towns and now we were entering rolling hills covered with wheat and sagebrush.

Startled by the noise of the train, cattle lumbered away from the tracks towards the top of a knoll where a herd of deer grazed. Two llamas lay in a field staring placidly, undisturbed by our presence. A lone coyote loped in the distance. Straining as we climbed into higher country, the train creaked and groaned. I could feel my mind expand, stimulated by the wide, open spaces.

After breakfast in the dining car, my husband walked to the

windowed observation car while I sat in our private room, dreaming and staring out the window, surrounded by books and papers.

At every meal in the dining room we shared tables with strangers: a passionate architect who designed libraries with fireplaces and cozy spots to read; a forty year old Alaskan truck driver whose boyfriend in Iowa read classics to her by telephone and inspired her to start college; a successful TV writer on his way back to Hollywood. Close to midnight we got off at the station in Flagstaff, Arizona. We had left Chicago thirty-three hours earlier.

The next day we drove to Mesa, Arizona to visit my husband's family. It was Thanksgiving and we planned to be there for a week. Intending to get a lot done, I came loaded with work — books, papers, and my appointment calendar. My husband's parents were quiet people and there was little conversation in the house so I had large blocks of time to think. I set myself up at a table in the walled-in patio, sat in my shorts and worked *on* my business, instead of *in* it.

This is how I spent part of my vacations for many years before I learned to leave work behind and replace business books with novels, proposals with knitting or drawing, and legal pads with journals. Now I know there are times you should work *in* the business, times you should work *on* the business, and times when you should not work at all.

The pressures to work *in* the business are enormous. You

spend most of your working hours immersed in tasks. You wait on customers, make products, orchestrate PR events, manage conferences, build/lease/sell property, design ads, write speeches/ newsletters/software, consult with or train/coach clients, program computers, conduct research, etc. If you're not careful you'll race from project to project and never slow down long enough to appreciate what you've accomplished or evaluate your outcomes. Like robots, you do what's right in front of you and get swallowed up by busywork.

Working *on* the business involves stepping out of everyday demands to look at the bigger picture and ask yourself: What's working? What isn't working? What should I do different? It involves dreaming about possibilities, ideas for products or services, and an exciting future. It involves planning how to re-structure your business, increase income, set and reach goals, and attract more clients/ customers. It involves thinking about the decisions you have to make, what business you're really in, and how to handle issues with employees. Many people consider it a luxury to take time to dream, plan, and think. I consider it critical to thriving.

Just because everyone else is insane and crazed, doesn't mean you have to be, too. The major reason we don't stop working is because we're afraid — afraid we'll lose money if we don't work 24/7. But if you incorporate working *on* the business as a practice, you'll shift from being reactive to proactive, get re-energized, and feel more centered and calm.

In my entrepreneurs' groups, members work on each other's business. They urged Bobbye to submit the company newsletter she wrote to a contest (it won an award), reminded Jen to find other major clients, helped Colin think through how to attract customers who own the high-end antiques he buys and sells, brainstormed with Stephanie on how to reach her target market, encouraged Tom to interview potential sub-contractors to meet the demands of his busy website design business, and helped Arnie begin to put in place an idea he's had for a long time for how to expand services to his clients. I'm convinced the work these members have done on their businesses is a major reason they've beaten the odds for survival and managed to thrive, even in tough economic times.

There's a price for not working *on* the business. A client I hadn't seen for a long time came in to talk about how scattered and frantic he felt. He confessed, "I never plan. I just react." I suggested he go to a café or library with his laptop and/or a pad of paper once a week so he could think without interruption about what he wants to accomplish and how to move his business forward.

"If you put your thoughts and ideas down on paper in black and white, it will reduce the swirl in your mind and give you the opportunity to look at everything with fresh eyes," I told him. As he talked about his concerns out loud, he sorted out many issues.

All he needed was to stop long enough to think.

Remember J.J., the musician who teaches drums and harmonica? A short story about him exemplifies how working *on* your business can boost your results. One December meeting when we were reviewing the past year, J.J. reported that this was the first time in many years he hadn't increased his income.

"What do you think happened?" I asked.

"You know, I didn't set goals last year. I'm not doing that again," he answered. In January he wrote ambitious goals and by the end of that year, he had increased his revenues again. It's not magic, even though it sounds like it. Goals are like a road map. Even if you don't accomplish them fully, you'll be further along than if you didn't have them. If you take your goals out of your head and enter them into your computer or write them down on paper, they'll feel more real and serve as a reminder every time you look at them.

You'll be tempted to consider it a waste of time to work *on* the business but it deserves your *attention* as well as your *intention*. Take care of your business the same way you do with anything else you love. It's just like performing regular maintenance on your car to retain its value and keep it running smoothly.

There's no time more perfect than the end of one year and the beginning of the next for working *on* the business. Here's a powerful four-step process you can use.

1. For the first step, review the past year in late December or early January and list all the failures, setbacks, and disappointments that occurred. Be honest. This will give you an opportunity to create a more mature relationship with failure, discover the lessons you've learned, and put in place practices or systems to prevent repeating mistakes. Be sure to forgive yourself (and anyone else involved), then put it all in the past where it belongs.

2. Next, review the past year again and list all the successes you experienced — the good things that happened, the great people who came into your life, and all you accomplished. Don't forget to include the gifts of insight or learning you received from failures. As you make your list, allow yourself to feel pleasure and gratitude. Then plan a celebration. Include anyone who was a part of your success so that you can acknowledge and thank them.

3. Now you're ready to take the third step and look at all the unfinished business from the past year, especially the loose ends that nag at you. List all of them. What do you know you will never do? Tell the truth. Cross it off your list and let it go. What do you commit to finish, and by when? Write it down. Include the dates and any supports or help you'll need to follow through.

After these steps you'll have the freedom and emotional space to dream about the New Year. This is the time to set heart-based goals. Getting a dental check-up or a colonoscopy does not qualify. They belong on a "To-Do" list. Heart-based goals should inspire passion and enthusiasm when you look at them. Maybe for you, it's a goal to take the family to a dude ranch this summer, or to learn to skydive, or to go to Italy and stay in a villa. Three goals are enough for one year.

The last step is to use poster board or a small page in your calendar to create a collage of pictures and words that serve as visual reminders of your goals. Just be sure to put it where you can look at it frequently.

I've done this process every year since I started my business. If you do it, I promise you'll go flying into the New Year with freedom and energy. It's a great way to take care of your business and you'll find yourself looking forward to it as an annual ritual.

Incorporating powerful practices into your business life will build a solid foundation for thriving.

Part III
Learn the Art of Thriving

Chapter 14
Manage Your Well-Being

I was in the middle of facilitating a workshop when I started to feel strange, a little light-headed, and oddly, the room seemed to be moving.

This was one of the first public workshops I offered as part of my new business. I did everything myself — designed it, advertised it, enrolled participants, made name tags, typed the attendance list, set up the room, greeted people as they arrived, and collected money. Then I began leading the workshop and as late arrivals showed up, interrupted what I was saying, ran to the back of the room to sign them in, and.... whew.

Now I wondered what was happening to me. Was I about to faint? Have a heart attack? My mind went blank. I paced back and forth and then asked the group to repeat back to me what I had just said. Several participants read from their notes but nothing registered in my mind. I made up an exercise to give them on the spot, ran to the bathroom, sat in the stall, and waited for whatever was happening to pass. After a while I felt better but still shaky. I managed to get through the rest of the workshop and convinced myself that this was a one-time event that would never happen again.

It wasn't. The next time I was in the middle of a speech in front of hundreds of people. Feeling faint, I abruptly ended the talk and walked off the stage. Again, I was okay after a while. I hoped this was the end of it. Then I started having episodes while walking in the city that felt as if buildings were moving and closing in on me. By now I was sure I knew what was wrong. I had an appointment already scheduled with my gynecologist and I attended filled with dread. I knew she would confirm my diagnosis: Cancer.

"I don't know, Robin. I can't find anything. I think it might be stress," she told me.

Clearly she was mistaken. On to my GP who listened to my symptoms, as well as my diagnosis, and in a kind voice asked what was going on in my life.

"Not much," I answered. "I've started a business, I've been working hard and I'm scared, that's all." A sob lodged in my throat and caught me by surprise.

"I think it's stress, Robin," he said.

"It can't be," I assured him. "I'm leading stress management workshops!"

He suggested I was having panic attacks and recommended I cut back on sugar and caffeine to eliminate jacking my system up and down. And, he prescribed rest.

I went home, climbed into bed, pulled the shades, took the phone off the hook, and slept on and off for days. I'd been so motivated since starting my business that I'd worked every day for two years straight, including weekends, with almost no break. For the first time, it was my show and I loved doing everything — choosing letterhead, writing brochures, designing workshops, networking, and giving speeches. I'd worked so hard because I was excited, and because I was too scared to slow down. I rarely asked for help.

My body had the wisdom to know that I needed to change my life. One of the first decisions I made was to take at least one full day a week off from work. I promised myself I wouldn't work on Sundays and gradually, over the years, I've added Saturdays, except for occasional weekend workshops. I've also scheduled longer vacations, including two sabbaticals (more about that later). Resting is like putting money in the bank. Just like professional athletes, we need to learn to pace ourselves and build in recovery time.

I've also learned to ask for help. Being fiercely independent is a major strength of self-employed people. It's also a liability. Whether you're reluctant to seek help because you have an elevated ego, are just plain stubborn, or have a scarcity mentality, it's dangerous to think you can do everything yourself. By taking on too much, you can end up burned out, and that will diminish results and kill off the vibrancy in your business. Even part-time help is valuable. It will help you take care of yourself and free you up to do what you need to do, nurture and grow your business.

Eliminating stress in a business is a pointless goal. All you can do is figure out how to reduce and manage it. Being an entrepreneur is often more mentally tiring than physically. Working without a break is not healthy. If you were to tell me you're exhausted, that you've put on weight, haven't had time to exercise, and haven't taken a day off in a year, I know from experience the problem is not the business. It's *you*. You need to learn to set boundaries and keep them. You need to take good care of yourself. It's important to build in time to get your mind totally off the business. Get out of your house or office and take walks, or grab a snooze, watch a movie, attend a concert, go exercise, play with the kids, or work on the house. There's a world out there. Go gain some perspective.

Remember the real bottom line? It's always about managing yourself. Learning to pace yourself and ask for help are two behaviors that lead to thriving. A third is to heed your own internal warning system. Fortunately, I had a wake-up call early in my business.

"I'm so lucky to be alive, "I whispered. Although the restaurant was crowded and noisy, we leaned into each other for privacy.

"Me too," she said. In an earlier conversation she had admitted she had a drinking problem when she was young. I revealed I did too, but at the time, we were sitting with a group of female friends and the conversation had veered off onto other "bad girl" confessions. Now we were by ourselves and this was our first opportunity to pick up the threads of that conversation again.

"I hid it so well that no one talked to me about it, warned me, or suggested I was playing with fire," I told her. I added that I drank secretly before I went out for dinner, suggested restaurants that served liquor (never mentioning that was the reason for the choice), and then continued to drink alone after I got home. I was seldom drunk, but got high every evening. Although no one knew, somewhere deep inside of me, an internal truing device set off an alarm that I was off-course and in deep trouble.

Still, after twenty-three years of drinking almost every day, I couldn't imagine quitting. I had solidly defended reasons why I should continue. How else would I relax after working hard all day? Or reward myself for all my hard work? Without alcohol, I wouldn't be able to fall asleep at night, be "cool," enjoy sex, or have fun at parties. I couldn't imagine stopping.

Then I started to have blackouts and shortly after noon, I began counting the hours until 5:00 PM when I could have a drink. I told myself that if I could wait that long, it meant I wasn't an alcoholic. I was moody and edgy. Dramas filled my life — unhappy relationships with men, arguments with my mother, and problems at work. I was certain that I wasn't to blame for any of it — "they" were.

My friend and I shivered as we shared risks we had taken full of alcoholic courage. One night close to midnight, after drinking and having an argument with my first husband (a stormy, brief, alcohol-filled marriage), I stomped out of the house, jumped on my motorcycle, and rode north for miles along Lake Shore Drive. On the way back I veered into another lane on Chicago's famous "S" curve without checking first and only afterwards, realized that a car could have been there. I was lucky.

We revealed other close encounters and then sat staring silently at each other. Alcohol free for many years now (since 1981 for me), we mused that no one would know our histories to look at us today. Here we were, happily married, middle class women with ordinary appearances and ordinary lives. We wondered how many other people, especially women, were out there hiding addictions.

I quit drinking a month before I became self-employed. If I

hadn't, I think my business would have eroded slowly over time, or imploded. Today, if I have a client who continues to struggle and coaching doesn't make a difference, I suspect that something else is going on. Often I discover that "something else" is an addiction.

One morning, sitting by a sun-filled window in a favorite café, I paused from writing in my journal, looked up, and spotted someone I knew waiting in line for coffee. I wondered what had happened to him. A few years ago my husband and I had asked him to give us an estimate for a home remodeling project because he came highly recommended as a good contractor. He showed up, looked around, listened to what we wanted, and expressed excitement about the project. Then he disappeared, didn't return calls and never followed through with a proposal. Finally we gave up and found someone else to do the job.

Today I watched him join a group of men at a nearby table and overheard snatches of their conversation. It all fell into place. It was obvious they'd just come from an Alcoholics Anonymous meeting. He had probably been drinking back then.

Trust me, being self-employed is challenging enough without having to deal with an addiction too. Alcohol and drugs are not antidotes for stress. Abuse of either will weaken your will, lessen your ability to keep attention on work, and threaten stable relationships. It leads to poor decisions and unnecessary risks, and fuels paranoia, depression, and feeling victimized.

You're the glue for your business. Like an athlete, you need to be in good shape. That means bringing integrity not only to your accounting practices but also to your body, mind, and spirit. Being successfully self-employed demands the best in you — the ability to focus, make sound decisions, take sane risks, and maintain a constancy of optimism. In fact, the opportunity to grow and develop as a human being may be the best gift you'll receive from being self-employed. Taking care of your well-being is a way to invest in your business, keep it healthy, and ensure thriving.

After study and experimentation, Positive Psychology professor and author, Martin Seligman suggests in his newest book, *Flourish*, that well-being is comprised of five elements: positive emotion (happiness), engagement (flow), relationships, meaning, and achievement. You can visit his website to learn more, see how you rate on numerous tests, and even do exercises to increase your sense of well-being. I believe there are very few life style options that give you a better chance to experience all of these components than creating and owning your own business. It may be your best bet. Just be careful to protect and nurture your business and yourself.

Chapter 15
Create Safety Nets

Chatting and laughing, eight people climbed the stairs to my living room. It was Friday morning and on the dining table next to hot coffee I had placed a homemade raspberry sour cream coffee cake. Usually I offered something more pedestrian like store-bought bagels and cream cheese, but today I had felt inspired.

Everyone sat in a circle, some curled up in chairs, others on the couch. It's not your typical business environment. Once a month, in this relaxed and intimate setting, I lead a support group for entrepreneurs comprised of members who range in age from early forties to mid sixties. No one is in a competing business and many members have been self-employed for more than ten years. If there is such a thing as a typical meeting, it includes celebration, a few tears, lively discussion, and a plethora of helpful ideas.

For a while, Angie attended this group. When she joined, she was in the late stage of working on plans for her store. At one memorable meeting she announced that she had finally opened the doors. Loud applause. Then in passing, she casually mentioned something about her husband. Husband?? Oh yes, she added, she had also gotten married this last month. More applause, more congratulations, and requests to see her ring followed. Married. Well, well.

"You know, it will help with insurance," she explained. Sure.

I knew that prior to opening her store she had had a long relationship with a great guy who had wanted to be married for a while. He had supported her every step of the way in this new journey and she had plenty of evidence that he was a solid partner. In my eyes, making a full-out commitment to her business had made it easier for her to make a commitment to him too.

At this meeting, Jane moaned as she checked in, "The kids are out of school, my aunt died and a contract cancelled...help!" I wasn't worried. I knew by the end of the morning she'd be ready to go again. Actually, these challenges were "small potatoes" for her compared to what she's confronted during her time with the group.

Hit by a tidal wave of personal and family issues, it began with a bee sting. She had a severe allergic reaction that threw her heart into erratic behavior for months and left her feeling weak and exhausted. Shortly after she recovered from that, she was diagnosed with breast cancer. Then just as she was almost healed from surgery and thought she was done, another lump was found and she had to have a second operation followed by radiation. Finally, she recovered and began to feel whole again. She treated herself to a solitary weekend retreat to think about the direction she wanted to take her business and returned feeling excited and energized by the new goals she had set. Then just as she was getting started on them, one of her two children was diagnosed with a life-threatening physical condition that required numerous consultations with doctors and a great deal of time and attention. And she had to handle much of it herself because she's a single mom.

Doesn't your heart go out to her? She was extremely grateful she had her own business because it gave her the flexibility to manage these traumatic events. Throughout it all, Jane managed to stay connected with her monthly group, a small band of people who loved and supported her, and provided an additional lifeline to that already offered by her family and friends.

I started support groups for entrepreneurs because I know from experience that being self-employed can sometimes be isolating. Although we may crave solitude at times to concentrate on work, especially when we're creating something new, too much time alone is not good. There's a danger of getting cut off from the world and stuck in our own ruts. And, because we have no one to hold us accountable, we can engage in the mischief of not keeping our word about deadlines and goals.

It's important to have people to share your accomplishments with — people who appreciate what it took. You also need people who are safe to talk to about failures and who will continue to challenge you to be your best. I believed that if I put the right group of entrepreneurs together in the same room, all that would happen and creative sparks would fly too. It's proven to be true. By the end of our meetings, people leave feeling energized and inspired. I've facilitated these groups for over twenty-seven years and I still look forward to the meetings.

It's no accident that 95% of my clients who have participated in these groups have had successful businesses. They haven't left their futures to chance and have recognized the importance of surrounding themselves with support. They're clear that asking for help doesn't mean they're weak. No one can know and do everything well — even you.

Don't worry if you don't know about a support group where you live. You may be the perfect person to start one or you can encourage someone else to do it. Just make sure you find or create a group that's different from a networking or leads group, although both happen naturally. A support group is not just for brainstorming either, even though members generate lots of ideas. Be sure to create a group that's based on a shared commitment to have a great life, not just a great business.

Create a space where entrepreneurs can crow unabashedly about successes, express serious doubts and the temptation to quit, admit to failures, struggle with challenges, be openly sad or discouraged, ask for advice, work their way through problems, receive feedback on plans and marketing materials, talk about family-related issues, get a dose of tough-love if needed, find out about resources, and give birth to exciting ideas. Anything related to being an entrepreneur is fair game. How can we possibly separate our lives into compartments, especially when we're self-employed?

We've walked members through the pain of lost contracts, trouble with the IRS, the death of parents and a spouse, debilitating illness, surgeries, taking care of children, marriages, births, sabbaticals, retirement, and everything else that a human life involves.

The support we end up giving each other might surprise you. For example, after Jane had dealt with one crisis after another that pulled her away from her business, she thought she should push herself to get back to work. She admitted she was worn out and really wanted to take the summer off but thought that would be the wrong thing to do. Instead, we encouraged her to do it. She returned from a badly needed rest ready to tackle what was next. Instead of driving herself, she took care of her well-being and allowed her enthusiasm to return naturally. It proved to be the right answer.

If you don't see any possibilities for this kind of group, look for people who live in your community and are self-employed and meet with them regularly for mutual support. Find a few people you can trust and talk honestly to about the challenges you're confronting, people who will support you to move past your fears, people who will help in the tough times but also celebrate with you in the great times. A woman who owns her own publishing company said she helped form a group of self-employed people in her community and they meet once a month for breakfast, just to talk. She loves it. If you want to form a more structured support group like I lead, I've included guidelines in the back of the book that you can use to do that.

When you work for a company, you don't have to make an effort to fill your social needs because coworkers are just down the hall. But when you're self-employed, especially if you work alone, it's up to you to make sure you have enough contact with people. Schedule coffee, breakfast or lunch with uplifting people and remember, even if you love your employees, they aren't a replacement for friends or colleagues.

Not everyone is a part of your safety net. Outside of your trusted support network, you need to use discernment about who you talk to and what you say about your business. It can be dangerous. One time a colleague I met on the street began our conversation by saying she was sorry to hear I was closing my business. "Where did you hear that?" I gasped. I figured out from her response that earlier in the week I had voiced discouragement about my business to an acquaintance at a professional meeting. I don't like to lie and pretend everything is fine when it isn't, but my too-open disclosure had clearly not been wise, especially with someone I didn't know well. I've even learned to be careful how I talk with my closest family members.

I married after being in business for eight years. In addition to paying for our wedding we took on the expense of buying a house and for the first time in my life I had a mortgage. Wouldn't you know that coincided with a time when my business slowed down? I was scared. One evening I told my new husband that I was afraid we weren't going to be able to pay the mortgage and we would lose the house. A couple of days later, I noticed he was quiet and moping. "What's wrong?" I asked apprehensive that he was unhappy in our marriage, of course.

"We're gonna' lose the house and have to move. I'm bummed."

"Where did you get that idea?" I asked.

"You told me your business was going under."

"Oh, don't worry. Everything's okay," I said breezily as I walked into the next room, happy about the new business that had come in yesterday.

I was fine but it took my husband longer to recover. I've had to learn to be careful not to enroll him in my fear. His life

experience has been different from mine. He's always been employed and has never been an entrepreneur. He doesn't understand what it's like or how quickly things can change. It's wrong
to drag him too much into my fears but it's equally as bad not
to let him know when things have improved. He's on to me now
and rolls with the punches when I start worrying. "You'll be fine.
You'll figure it out. You've been here before," he advises.

An experience one of my clients had reinforces this cau-
tion to be careful who you talk to, especially in the early stages
of your business. Sandra, a new business owner who was not sure
how to handle something that had come up with her work, asked
for advice from a woman who was well established in the same
field, successful, and much more experienced. By the time the call
ended, Sandra was totally deflated. Her colleague was not only
rude and mean, she also berated Sandra for how she had designed
her business and suggested she had done everything wrong. It
took a lot of support from group members before Sandra could
find her grounding again. We encouraged her to remain true to
herself, continue to trust herself, and remember that there are a
lot of ways to run a business, not just one right way.

Support can take a lot of different forms and isn't limited to
conversations. It can come from books, CDs, and videos, any me-
dium that inspires and motivates you. Remember my story about
my marketing failure at a trade show and how I didn't generate

one enrollment for my workshops from all that effort? Well, I was still moping two weeks later when I ran into my friend Ron. It was late on a Friday afternoon. Always smiling and upbeat, Ron was a successful salesman.

"How's it going?" he asked. I told him about my recent debacle and admitted I was discouraged.

"I don't know what to do," I said.

"Wait a minute," he said and ran to his car parked nearby. He opened the trunk and handed me a set of audiotapes called *"The Psychology of Winning"* by Denis Waitley.

"Listen to this. It will make a difference," he urged. Even though I was skeptical, I borrowed them because I trusted Ron. That weekend because I didn't feel like being around people and had no plans, I had plenty of time to listen. There were twenty tapes. After dinner on Friday night, I grabbed a legal pad of paper and started taking notes. For the following two days, in between laundry, grocery shopping, cooking, and running errands, I sat at the dining room table listening and writing.

On Friday evening I had begun slumped in my chair. By Saturday afternoon I managed to sit up straight. And by Sunday, after finishing the tapes, I stood tall knowing that my marketing plan for the workshops had been a complete failure but *I* was not. It was a powerful distinction. On Monday I was ready to get to work again.

That was my introduction to motivational recordings. I've discovered they're a vast improvement to the conversation in my own mind when I'm in a funk. Over the years I've listened to many and recommended them to clients. I've also read motivational books and attended numerous personal growth seminars and workshops, all of which have inspired me to stay in the game.

If you surround yourself with support, you'll have a safety net and will increase your odds for surviving and moving right on to thriving.

Chapter 16
Enjoy All the Perks

"I'm so tired. All I want to do is take the summer off," I whined as we trudged back to the office from another sales appointment. My energy reserves were stuck on empty. It was June, the start of summer, and I was longing to play.

"Then, do it," she said. I stopped right in the middle of the sidewalk and stared at my employee.

"Really?"

"Really," she said, completely reversing roles as she gave me permission.

After thirteen years in business, I wanted a break — a long one. On my last vacation I'd barely begun to unwind before it was time to return to work.

Over the years, I had encouraged many clients to take as

much time off as they needed, especially in between losing jobs and starting new ones. "Tell people you're taking a sabbatical," I had advised. But the truth is, I hadn't taken one myself because I was afraid. What if my business died? That day I had an even scarier thought; if I don't do it, will my spirit die?

My clients always loved their sabbaticals. They used time off to slow down... sleep late and take naps...travel to places they'd dreamed about...spend leisurely time with family and friends... jump into a mountain of untouched books and read to their heart's content...pursue hobbies in depth...conduct exciting research...be adventurous and scale high peaks, go on a trek or safari, or run a marathon...or just let the days unfold without a plan.

I decided to take ten weeks off with no agenda. My only goals? To buy a new car (fun) and clean closets (mindless and satisfying). I wrote daily in my journal and one day after I asked myself again what I should do next in my work/life, I swear a bolt of energy rushed through my body into my arm and the words, "Write your book" showed up on the page. I took the message seriously and it led to *No More Blue Mondays/Four Keys to Finding Fulfillment at Work*, published in 1999. It also began a love affair with writing that has turned into a lasting passion.

I would have taken a third month off from work if I hadn't been a worrywart about money but I had promised to return by fall and I felt good. My business had survived with help from my employee who had kept things going. The personal benefits of this break lasted for eight years and then my husband retired. That changed everything.

I felt torn working in my office at 10:00 in the morning while he was sitting upstairs still drinking coffee, reading the newspaper, and easing into a relaxed day. I was tired. I had been in business for twenty-one years, was sixty-one years old, and wondered if I should retire too. Time off would give me a chance to see what that life might be like.

"Take a whole year off," an internal voice urged.

Whoa. Way too scary. I countered with three months.

"Too short," she retorted.

I upped it to six months.

"What I really want is a year," she stubbornly insisted.

I scoured the budget, reworked numbers, and stared at money I'd saved for a rainy day. Maybe *this* was that rainy day. I ended up designing a year's sabbatical with only twenty per cent of my time filled with work. When I wasn't afraid, I was excited.

I began this sabbatical in January, the time of year in the Midwest when we wake up in the dark and the sun slips to the horizon by four o'clock in the afternoon. Like furry animals, we hibernate. For the first two months, in the short amount of time pale light was available, I sat indoors at a card table working on jigsaw puzzles. As soon as I sat down, my mind entered a Zen-like state. It was perfect. Pure pleasure. No redeeming value or purpose. No goals or bottom line to meet. Each day my body unwound a little more, like a tightly knotted ball of yarn unraveling.

That fall my husband and I fulfilled a dream. We towed our trailer out west and camped for six weeks in places we'd always wanted to see: Yellow Stone National Park, The Grand Tetons, and the Badlands of South Dakota. During the year, I also fulfilled creative yearnings by attending writing, cooking, and drawing classes. I added Yoga as a practice. I rested and slowed down. It was just what I needed.

Close to the end of the year I knew I was not ready to retire. I felt restless and missed my clients. I decided to work part-time so I could continue to write and participate in two volunteer projects I loved. Although I had no employee to take care of my business during this sabbatical, shortly after I sent a newsletter out announcing I was back, I was busy again.

One of the greatest perks of being a business owner is that you can choose to take long vacations. Are you yearning for time off but worried it will hurt your business?

It will be the opposite. It actually helped my business rather than hurt it because I returned feeling refreshed and reinvigorated. Time off will prove to be a way to take good care of the heart and soul of your business — *you*. A real vacation means you don't check in with the office, make calls on your cell phone, send emails or text messages, or work on the computer. Instead, you're fully present to whatever you're doing at the moment – hanging out with family/friends or enjoying your solitude, reading books, taking naps, traveling, climbing mountains, running marathons, or attending classes that interest you. Ultimately, I discovered that if I allowed myself a complete break, I returned to work with an altered mindset, feeling refreshed and ready to dive in again.

If you're self-employed, along with the opportunity to take serious vacations, you have lots of other perks. They may not match exactly the corporate perks you left behind in paid employment but in my eyes, they're stellar. You'll never be told what your next assignment will be. Instead, you can design, attract, or go after the work you want, serve clients you love or enjoy being around, and say "no" to toxic people and situations. You'll never be fired or laid off. And if you want to slow down, you can work part-time and still do what you love. You're the boss. Remember? Ahem.

You'll never be bored for long. You can always create something new. And when you need time to handle personal and family issues, you don't have to ask permission for time off or worry about what will happen to your job. I especially appreciated the flexibility I had as a business owner when my mother was dying. Her health declined gradually over seven months. Because she lived seven hundred and fifty miles away, the telephone was our lifeline. I talked to her almost every day in the privacy of my living room, feeling our love flow through the wires and fill the room. I visited frequently for long weekends and close to her death, stayed for a month to help her make the transition from assisted living to a nursing home. I still wonder how I would have handled this if I had been employed. Being my own boss made it much easier.

If you're self-employed at sixty-five, you won't get sidelined, shoved into a corner, or replaced by a younger person with a tenth of your experience who will be paid half your salary. I've noticed that my clients and friends who own their own businesses are happy continuing to work while people who are employed complain they can't get out fast enough.

If you do retire and find playing golf or doing crossword puzzles is not enough, or you begin to focus on body parts, you'll probably welcome the opportunity to work late into your life. Like me, you may discover that not working leads to an existential crisis: Why am I alive? What use am I to anyone? Work provides a focus for your life, social connections, opportunities for achievement, and engagement in doing something you love – all of which contribute to a sense of well-being.

Remind yourself to enjoy the perks. Having the freedom to

design a life you love is a major reason why you chose to be self-employed in the first place. If you take advantage of this freedom and remember you're choosing to thrive on your own terms, you'll remain engaged for the long haul.

And that's what you want, isn't it?

Chapter 17
Make Authentic Choices

Business was growing and we were humming. I was starting to feel more confident and then the building I lived and worked in was sold with no warning. The new owner announced that all the units would be converted to condominiums. After eight years in the same location I needed to find a new office and a new home, all at once. Lots of decisions. Lots of expenses. Where to locate your work is one of the four major decisions you'll have to make in the lifetime of a business and it's one you may confront more than once.

Luckily, my husband and I found a small townhouse for our home in a nearby suburb. I also located a rental space in the city for our office in a newly developing area populated by artists, graphic and interior designers, videographers, and antique dealers. Located an easy walk from shops, restaurants, and offices on Michigan Avenue, it had a kitchen, reception area, three interior offices, and a large room lined with windows on one side, a great setting for workshops. Exposed beams and red brick walls gave it a cozy, loft-like feel. I had three full-time employees and one part-time. It was the perfect size for us.

Now I felt sure I was on my way to meeting my picture of success, but only three years later I was wondering why I wasn't happy. This was what I'd always wanted, wasn't it? My original vision had been to build a big business. Now I questioned it. I felt tense and anxious, worried about paying the bills. Then a key employee left unexpectedly to join a competitor. We were too small to absorb the loss of one person easily and I took it as a setback and personal failure. I vacillated between hiring someone to replace her and renting the vacant office, and ended up doing neither.

At first I had been thrilled with our space but now rent and salaries hung like a dark cloud over me. It began to feel like a burden. I had deliberately kept client fees low so I could work with a wide range of people in the public part of my business (workshops and one-on-one coaching) but that meant I had to do constant marketing and selling to supply the numbers we needed. Or, I had to take on corporate work (training and consulting) to bring in enough income, but this was not my first love. Added to that,

I found managing people required a lot of attention and energy, even with a small staff.

I had always urged my clients to follow their hearts and now I had moved further away from my own. I felt inauthentic and increasingly constrained by the very structures I had created.

Work was not fun any more. Towards the end of our five-year lease, I reluctantly began looking for another office. I searched on and off for months. Nothing was right: wrong location, bad floor plans or high rent.

Finally I told the truth. I didn't want to sign another long-term lease on a large office. I wanted to simplify my business and my life. I pared back to one employee, rented an office for her in a shared office facility and moved my work into my town-house where I had a perfect setup for a home office. The two of us handled administrative details without secretarial help and returned to using hotel spaces for workshops. We talked by telephone every day and saw each other often, but it was not a good situation for her so it was understandable when she announced she was leaving. After fourteen years in business I had come full circle and returned to working by myself at home again.

Your business may grow, contract, or shift in shape. Over thirty years of being self-employed, I've had to relocate my business numerous times. I've worked from home, sublet and rented offices, and used a shared office facility. Each of these decisions was the right one at the time.

I remember meeting with a woman who had been in business successfully for many years. She was frantic about money because her business had slowed dramatically due to the recession (and her own lethargy). When I asked her about expenses, she said she paid $1,200.00 a month to rent an office in a prestigious building. She acknowledged that she didn't need the space because she no longer had employees, usually visited clients in their settings, and with a computer and cell phone, could work from almost anywhere. I suggested she move her business into her home to reduce a significant amount of stress in her life. It became clear she wasn't willing to do this, primarily because of her ego, and it didn't surprise me when she never followed through with another appointment.

Working at home is the smartest thing you can do if it fits your business. You'll have a flexible lifestyle and save time, energy, and money. It's been seventeen years since I moved my office back into my home and I love working here. I appreciate the ease it grants in my life and the periods of time I have alone for writing, reading, and thinking. My clients like meeting here too and comment on how peaceful it is. When I need to be around more people, I seek them out to schmooze or collaborate with on joint ventures or projects.

But a home office is not for everyone. If you get sidetracked playing with the kids, watching TV, or puttering around the house, you need to relocate your office. If your work spills into the living room, dining room, and kitchen, and you can never get away from it, it's time to go. If the house is crowded with employees and it's driving the people you live with crazy, or no one in your family respects the privacy of your workspace and dumps everything on your desk, or you feel lonely and need to be around people, find a space outside your home.

You'll know if and when the time is right to make this move. The decision shouldn't always hinge on money but you'll probably more than make up for the added expense by being more productive. Just seeing your business name on a building directory can be a powerful motivator to grow your business.

Thinking about office space reminds me of my client, Michael. Although he's a natural leader, he's never recognized it in himself and would describe himself as an accidental entrepreneur. Michael began as a rigger, work that requires climbing up on scaffolds and hanging thousands of pounds of lighting for concerts, plays, and business events. It takes great skill and with all that heavy equipment hanging over peoples' heads, there's no room for mistakes.

Before he started his own business, he was a "roadie" for many years and toured with famous performers, including Michael Jackson. He earned a reputation for competence and safety. When he married, he stopped traveling. He bought a little equipment here and there, stored it in a warehouse in the city, began to hire other riggers to work with him, and ran his business from a home office in the suburbs.

He couldn't have predicted how optimal this arrangement would be until his wife became ill. With the help of his family, Michael ran his business and took care of her at home until she died. After that, he knew he needed to move his business out of his home, but for a long time he lacked the energy to even think about it. All he could do was put one foot in front of the other.

Some time later Michael told me, "I want to do something different with my life. I'm ready to sell my business."

"There's a problem here," I said. "Your business is in your head and your office is in your home. How are you going to sell it? You need to move your business out and put what's in your head into a computer."

It took a while to make the commitment, but eventually he rented a larger warehouse, moved his office and equipment into it, hired administrative help and additional riggers, set up systems, and ended up growing his business.

It's been eighteen years since he started his own venture. Today he has the largest rigging business in the Midwest and recently hired a CEO to run the day-to-day operations. He also sold the house that was filled with sad memories and moved to the city into a home filled with light and decks for gardens.

In addition to choosing a location, a second major decision you'll confront as an entrepreneur is whether to grow your business or stay small. The mantra, "Bigger is better," may drive most business in this country, but it may not be your mantra. You might not be willing to do what it takes to become big and although it generally leads to increased revenue, exciting challenges, and greater impact, it can also lead to higher overhead, additional employees, and more complex problems. You have to decide what you want and what you can handle with grace and ease.

Ultimately, you may discover that having a big business is not what you thought it would be. It might take you further away from what you love to do and undermine the lifestyle you want.

There are ways to continue growing that don't include hiring more people. You can go deeper rather than wider. You can become an expert, a sought-after speaker, or an author of books and articles. You can expand your work with clients by offering new products or services. You can commit to a new level of excellence. You can seek out new challenges. The key to having a vibrant business is to remain engaged, and that doesn't depend on size.

There are also ways to grow that don't depend on full-time help. A colleague of mine designed and leads a popular workshop inside large corporations. She's great at generating contracts. In fact, she's too busy. If she decided to train other people to facilitate her workshops, she could grow her business, reduce traveling, spend more time with her family, and still reach more people. This could be a good solution but she would have to be willing to give up some control and so far, she hasn't been.

It's always a knotty problem as a small business owner to figure out how to get all the work done if you remain small. It feels like a big risk to hire help and you may worry about reducing income in the short term but ultimately it should support growth and increase revenues. Even part-time help can provide a huge boost.

The third major decision you'll need to make is whether you should own the business by yourself or take on a partner/partners. My observation is that many people start businesses by themselves and only think about taking on a partner when they're in trouble. Usually that trouble is running out of money. This is the worst time, and reason, to look for a partner. You're vulnerable and you'll be tempted to give away too much. The relationship may end up without parity and if you've given your blood, sweat and tears to get a business up and running, there's no way someone can compensate for that. If you do take on a partner, make sure the division of ownership reflects what you've already put into it. You'll have a greater chance of succeeding with a partner if you find someone right at the beginning of the business, someone with complimentary skills.

Business partnerships are like marriages without the sex (a few businesses even include that dynamic). They have all the same drama and intensity. A good partnership is not easy and takes hard work. Like a marriage, when a partnership is good, it's great, and when it's not, it's miserable. Think very carefully before you take this step. Try dating first by working on some projects together. Talk out issues as they come up. No matter how much you trust a person, get a written agreement and hire a lawyer to review it and protect your interests. Remember you can always form temporary partnerships through joint ventures or shared projects.

The fourth major decision you'll confront as an entrepreneur is how you define success. Will it be in terms of income, number of employees or clients, office size and appearance, who your clients are, or how much income you make? Or will you measure your success by your impact on clients or customers, the brilliance of your work, ease of your life, amount of freedom you have, your feeling of satisfaction at the end of the day, the passion you feel for your work, the time you have for yourself and/or with children, family and friends, or the flexibility you enjoy in your life? Or will it be some combination of these? You'll have to decide what feels right to you.

There are no formulas you can use to make these decisions. It's a matter of listening to yourself and respecting your intuition. Pay attention to how the choices you're considering affect your energy and enthusiasm and think about probable consequences.

Here are four questions you can use as guidelines when you

make these decisions. With each option, ask yourself, if I make this choice:

1. Will I continue to thrive and have a life I love?
2. Will my business still be vibrant?
3. Will I remain true to myself?
4. Will I be acting from my heart or my ego?

Taking direction from your ego is dangerous and leaves you vulnerable. Drawing on your internal wisdom for guidance will allow you to remain authentic and grounded, but it takes courage and strength to honor it.

There is probably no harder task than to remain true to yourself. Your commitment to this goal will be tested each time you're confronted with these major decisions. A good solid choice made thoughtfully and wisely will support living an authentic life.

Chapter 18
Stay Fully Engaged

After weighing in at Weight Watchers, I stopped for a big breakfast at Al's Restaurant — eggs over easy, crisp bacon, coffee, and rye toast. (Oh come on, probably all Weight Watchers do this after a weigh-in.) I chose to sit at the counter to avoid a ten-minute wait for a table. The place was jumping, filled with a potpourri of people including male and female, young, old, professional, working class, Hispanic, Afro-American, and Caucasian. Lots of families. Lots of kids. Great energy.

Al's used to be located across the street. I asked the man sitting on the stool next to me if he remembered it. "Yeah, it was a dump," he said. He was right. It had been seedy-looking, a little creepy to tell you the truth. The exterior was crumbling and the interior was dark, jammed with worn-out tables and chairs and a short, scarred counter. Even though the food was good, I only had the courage to eat there once.

"I was there for thirty years," the waitress commented, refilling my coffee. "There was only two of us." Today I counted five waitresses, two bus boys, and several cooks.

Six years ago, at the age of fifty, Al opened this new restaurant kitty corner to the old one. It's four times larger. He remodeled what was previously a dry cleaning pick-up store into a bright, cheery restaurant with modern booths, new tables and chairs, a long counter that seats eight people, and hanging plants. Light streams in through windows on two sides.

As I left, I stopped to chat with Al. He stood at the cash register, baseball cap on, reading glasses sliding down his nose.

"This is fabulous," I said. "Have you ever had a moment's regret about making the move?"

He peered over his glasses and answered, "No," with a huge smile but when I congratulated him on taking a big risk, he downplayed it. "Oh, it's just across the street from the old one and everyone around here knew me already."

Today Al was having a great time but I remember the tension and fear on his face in the early days of the move. I bet the past several years haven't been easy with the recession. He's probably had some tough moments since he moved. But here he is, someone who took a chance on himself, added spice to his

159

life, and is fully engaged.

But what if years later, despite all the benefits of being your own boss, you find yourself whining again? Not as much as when you were employed of course but still, whining is whining. When you start a business, you think you'll always love your work. You never think you'll get tired, bored, or sick to death of it but what if you become downhearted, hit a slump, or you're just done?

That's the time to use the best entrepreneurial perk of all: your power to change things. After all, you're in charge. This is the time to step back and ask yourself: what's true for me right now?

Are you still motivated by the five fierce desires: to be your own boss, do the work you want to do, express your creativity, design your own life, and earn as much money as you can through your own efforts? If the answer is yes, then what's missing or changed? If the answer is no, what's next?

Perhaps you haven't caught up with your own life and your priorities are different now. Maybe you have a spouse, partner, or children to consider for the first time, or you're a new grandparent. You could be at an age when you feel an increased sense of urgency to fulfill unmet dreams or you're burned out because you inadvertently slid from being enthusiastic into being driven. Maybe you're disappointed or discouraged, or mired down in toxic relationships with partners or employees. Sometimes the structures you design for a business become suffocating or outmoded and you can end up feeling victimized by your own creations.

Many entrepreneurs love starting something but find it hard to stick with it once everything is humming. You may need to create new challenges for yourself. Even small ones can make a difference. If you're feeling bored by everyday tasks, offer a sale or special promotion. It can be exciting not only for your customers, but more importantly for you. It's a new game to play. Maybe you're still trying to do everything by yourself. Or you're just tired. Or, you need to take a risk, like Al did with his restaurant, or tackle learning something new. Whatever your reason for whining, this is the time for renewal, for you to remember that you can streamline, simplify, or redesign your business. After all, you're the boss.

Andy is a client who got bogged down by his own resistance to change. After growing a computer technology business and being in a managerial role for many years, he knew his technical skills were outdated but he was afraid updating them would be too difficult. He rationalized that it was okay to rely on younger employees to do this work, but the truth was he felt out of the loop and his self-esteem suffered. Finally he began to watch training CDs. He remembered that the way he learned best was visually and he genuinely enjoyed them. He discovered that the hardest part was getting started and the technology itself wasn't nearly as difficult as he had thought. He got in touch with his love of learning again. Overcoming his resistance freed up energy and his self-confidence grew as he increased his knowledge and skill. He felt re-engaged with his business. This was the beginning of a renaissance for him. Since then, he's been excited about one new project after another.

You can tell when a business owner is mired in resignation, is robbing the business financially, is totally unconscious, or has given up, can't you? The telltale signs are everywhere: unruly stacks of papers dumped on every surface, chairs with cracked leather or ripped cloth seats, faded or chipped paint, lights or letters missing in exterior signs, stagnant air, and lethargic, unresponsive, gum-smacking employees. If this describes your business, turn it around. Clean up the office, replace the furniture, paint the walls, fix the signs, and hire new help.

Look at what inspired you originally. Does it still? Or, do you need a new vision with updated goals? Sometimes simply re-writing your goals is enough to start your energy flowing again. It's rarely a question of whether to remain self-employed or get a job; it's what to do next to feel re-invigorated and re-engaged in your business. Should you attend a new training in your field or a personal growth workshop to feel inspired again? Do you need to spend more time with people who are turned on by their work and optimistic? What will make a difference?

Tell the truth about whatever is going on. This will give you a powerful place to begin. From there, you'll see what actions you need to take and as soon as you get into motion, you'll feel inspired again. Every time I've hit a point in my business when I felt discouraged, disengaged or just blah, I've asked myself, what's the truth here? Then I've gotten back on track. So can you. Here's what Sara did.

"After our appointment, I cried all the way home," she wrote in an email to me. (Darn, I hate when that happens. And, it was a two-hour drive.) I felt sure the tears were due more to relief than sadness. Sara has been a self-employed artist for twenty years. At the time she began attending one of my entrepreneurs' groups, she was running a business offering faux finishes for homes and businesses. She had just turned fifty (a big decision-making year) and decided she no longer wanted to climb ladders to paint ceilings and walls. But neither did she feel inspired by the thought of hiring and training other people. She didn't know what she wanted to do next.

Then two big things happened in her life. The economy went into a tailspin slowing her business dramatically and her father became seriously ill. Sara considered the slowdown a blessing because it allowed her to spend more time with him before he died and it also gave her time to think.

At the meeting with me that preceded all those tears, she had talked about wanting to create a different future that would allow her to work as a consultant and bring the creative process to businesses and individuals.

"It might be wise to return to school and get an advanced degree," I suggested. That's what started the tears. She said she would have to complete a BA before she even began a Master's Degree because she had been told the college degree she had earned in Canada was not recognized in the United States. She admitted that this had been an incompletion for her for many years and now she was ready to do something about it.

We agreed that she should apply to great schools. Once she started the process, her spirits lifted and she was excited. The application process turned out to be transformational. Sara discovered that someone had given her the wrong information years ago and that her college degree was recognized here in the States. She also got great feedback on her portfolio from one of the best art schools in the country. In the end, she decided she didn't want a higher degree. Instead, she signed up for a yearlong workshop on creativity led by a famous teacher. It took place over four weekends and at the first one she attended Sara came up with an idea for a new business. Now she's focused on teaching artists how to start and grow a business and make a living, a perfect fit for her, a perfect audience, and a perfect leveraging of her experience and wisdom. She's on fire again.

Are you up for renewal? If you're lethargic and have lost your inspiration, it's time to light the fires again.

"I've lost my passion," complained the polished shoes, expensive suit, crisp white shirt, perfect tie, and trim haircut sitting opposite me. I couldn't find the human being behind the carefully constructed image.

After an hour of asking my first-time client the kind of questions that usually open things up (e.g., If you could have it any way you wanted, how would it look? What do you care about? Where's the juice for you?), and receiving only terse replies that led nowhere, I concluded he was smug, guarded, and not open to change. He proclaimed that he wanted to be more engaged in his work/life but clearly he also didn't want his world upset in any way.

"You're way too comfortable," I challenged him.

"Really, you think so?" he responded with a polite smile. His eyes never changed, remaining cool, unreadable. Unfortunately, he's a guy who's lost his bearings. I bet he was excited when he began his business but now many years later, he's achieved all his goals and has everything he needs and wants — money, prestige, work that takes him all over the world, even a few volunteer projects he likes. What he doesn't have are juicy goals in front of him. He's a self-satisfied partner in a successful business. To light the fires again, he needs to stop waiting for something to come along to excite him and be responsible for lighting up his own life.

One of the entrepreneurs' groups I facilitate is filled with members who have been in business for ten years or more. They're in the process of redefining themselves and their work. Some are ready to take their business to a new level, either in terms of expansion or excellence, while others have recognized that the world has changed and they have to change too or they'll be left behind. When they joined the group, most were bored, restless, and wondered if they were done with the focus they originally started with, but none of them wanted to stop being self-employed. Keith is an example.

For twenty years he ran a successful photography business shooting weddings. Although he had built a great base of business and was earning well, he had reached a point where he wanted to branch out and do something different. He knew the field of videography was changing dramatically and was aware of the impact of YouTube. He updated his skills and decided to focus on helping companies create effective videos. It required a totally different mindset and marketing plan. In essence, he started a new business.

The recession hit at the same time and it has taken Keith a while to lay the groundwork but he's finally gaining some traction and is booking more company clients. Recently he had an assignment where he knocked the ball out of the park — he wrote, choreographed, and filmed a video for a company-wide conference. At the same time that it communicated an important message, it was hilarious and fun. Everyone loved it. He was able to use all his past experience as an actor, his creative abilities, and his expertise behind a camera. He's excited now about creating a whole new future.

If you're willing to be flexible and make changes, you can stay true to yourself and remain engaged in your business for the long haul. It's not too late if you're over fifty to regenerate a great life. In fact, like many late bloomers I know, you may discover the best is still ahead.

Chapter 19
Savor Late Blooming

"You're a few years ahead of me, so what do you advise?" Paul asked.

"Learn to pace yourself," I answered.

I was schmoozing with a colleague at Ina's again and this time I had the gingerbread pancakes with lemon sauce.

My friendship with Paul has spanned many years and we've been partners in two joint ventures inside companies. He's been successfully self-employed as a Human Resources consultant for many years. He'll be sixty-three soon and is still excited about his work. He could have developed his consulting into a large business but chose not to and has remained close to the work he loves — coaching executive-level clients. Today his eyes lit up as he described the niche he's found. As he talked, I was struck again by the big dividends gained by staying true to yourself.

Before we parted, he commented that being in his sixties was different than any previous age. He felt an urgency now to do all the things he'd previously postponed — traveling, attending a film class, and taking cooking lessons. He wanted to slow down and round out his life. I understood.

I'm in my seventies and still love having my own business. I don't get stopped by my age very often, but I'm learning to be respectful of it. I recognize that it shapes how I work. For instance, I only do the things I genuinely like and instead of putting my efforts towards building a big business, I focus on deepening my relationship with my clients.

As I told Paul, I pace myself. Sometimes in the middle of the day I take a break and curl up with a novel or indulge my obsession with jig saw puzzles, a Zen-like meditation for me. Some days I work long hours but often I start late in the morning and stop at four o'clock. I've made time in my life to volunteer, pursue my passion for creative writing, and hang out with family and friends.

One of the best parts of being older is that I've let go of trying to prove myself, so I feel free to tell clients that I don't schedule appointments on the weekend, prefer meetings during the day and evening sessions that start no later than 6 PM. This year I also announced that I was taking off the whole month of July. My clients' response? "Good for you."

Recently I've had the thought that if I decide to work for only ten or eleven months a year, I'll feel enthusiastic about continuing my business for a long time into the future. A huge benefit of being self-employed is that it allows you to re-design your life whenever you want or need to do it.

If you're fifty or older, deciding to be an entrepreneur is a great choice because at that age, it's natural to want to control your own destiny. You'll also bring experience, maturity, and wisdom to whatever you do. Yes, it's a risk but it's a life-affirming one. Whether you become self-employed for the first time or reinvent an existing business, it will be enlivening.

You may be surprised to discover that your biggest hurdle to starting a business will be your own prejudice about age. We live in a culture that idolizes youth and devalues, minimizes, and belittles older people. It's hard not to buy into that negativity yourself. A test administered by a department at Harvard University that uses visual associations and "...allows you to see the truth even if you are unable or unwilling to know of your own biases consciously," reveals that one of the most important findings is "... that implicit biases are pervasive. For example over 80% of respondents show negativity toward the elderly compared to the young..." You may have to move past your own bigotry to allow yourself to blossom late in your life. As my friend Monica says, "People pay way too much attention to age — it doesn't mean what they think it does." She should know.

In her fifties she moved to Mexico to start a whole new life as an entrepreneur. She laid the groundwork for this transition for years while she was working full time. She already knew what it took to have a business because earlier in her life, she had been self-employed for a while. She loved being on her own but in response to life circumstances, she took a job for six years as a managing editor and worked inside a company. In her spare time she wrote screenplays, short stories and essays, and designed several web sites that had the potential to generate income. She also studied Spanish and researched places to live in Mexico.

When her company was hit hard by the recession, she was let go, along with many other employees. Instead of being in despair, Monica considered it a gift. She felt liberated. Now she could focus her energies on her own projects. She discovered a community of artists in a small town in Mexico, rented a house and moved there in 2009. After taking a few months off to adjust to her new life, she began her business. Since then she has co-authored a book about medical services for people who are considering moving to Mexico, generated individual writing/editing clients, and worked on projects her past employer has given her. She's currently exploring how to get a book of short stories published. She can run her creative business from anywhere. She's been scared, uncertain, excited, and energized; in other words, fully alive.

Thrive

As you age, it's hard not to buy into the vigorously promoted idea that you should retire to an unending vacation. A lifestyle without work may fit some people, but for many reasons it may not be right for you. You may need or want to work and as a coach, here is the question I pose to you: Retire to what? Most people retire *from* something, not *to* something. Wouldn't it be great if your retirement were exciting and totally engaging?

Becoming self-employed may be the answer, especially if you have a strong desire to contribute, enjoy starting things, want to create and/or build something, or yearn to design a lifestyle you love. Depending on your business, you can continue to work as long as you're interested, healthy, and vital. Many artists have worked into their nineties and recently I read a rave review about a concert given by Tony Bennett. The critic wrote that he's "at the top of his game" at age 85. My brother is a self-employed lawyer with two offices. Now in his mid-seventies, he told me he has cut back from working six days a week to five, but I doubt it. I suspect he also works at home on the weekends.

I understand if you have concerns related to being older. It's true that as you age your energy changes and you may be through with many activities like schlepping materials, traveling all over the country, creating scores of spreadsheets, or reviewing dense insurance reports. Now is the time to focus on the things you really love to do and eliminate or delegate as much of the rest as you can.

It means you'll have to set priorities, but that's always good.

Yes, it's hard to keep up with a constantly changing world, especially with technological advances, but it's hard for everyone, including younger people. You don't have to master all of it, just enough to run your business successfully. As a business owner, you may feel like you'll never finish all the work you have to do. It's true. You won't. You may also feel like you'll never catch up with all the rapid changes. It's true. You won't. Both of them come with the territory. As the kids say, "get over it." Just hold these thoughts lightly and do your best each day.

I'm willing to bet that your biggest challenge once you're in business will not be what you think. It will be managing your ego. If this is your first venture on your own, you'll soon realize that being self-employed is a whole new ballgame. Although you may be highly experienced in an area, maybe even an expert, you'll be a beginner at getting a business up and running and turning it into a successful venture. It may be hard to allow yourself to be a novice again, make mistakes, and remain open to learning. Although you're probably not used to it, you'll need to be humble and reach out for guidance and support. Trying to do it alone is a big mistake. And, although you may be used to operating in a large enterprise, here's a word of advice: don't try to start big. Here's what happened to one of my clients.

Terry was in his early fifties when he left an executive

position and a long career in one industry. The only thing he was certain about was that he didn't want to go back to that work again. He spent a long time exploring what he wanted to do next and in the process came up with an idea for a product for athletes. It arose naturally from his experience as a passionate ultramarathon runner. Everyone who saw it, or heard Terry talk about it, thought it was a winner.

I encouraged him to start small. He had the skills to make the product himself and could do it in his basement. I suggested first selling it at fairs and races but a friend advised him to do a national launch as soon as possible to avoid having the idea stolen. So he went for it in a big way and invested a lot of money.

He found himself on a steep learning curve. Designing and getting a product to market was entirely new to him. Before he could get it done, he ran out of money and created a mound of debt. He was forced to take a consulting job for several months to meet living expenses. Fortunately this work was a good fit and he managed to keep his business idea alive while doing it. In the meantime, he formed two different partnerships, one designing and managing local foot races and the other, creating an ultramarathon in Utah. He has clearly found his calling as a race director, work that is based on a passion. He's also found a way to generate income while he continues to work on getting his product into the marketplace.

I know Terry will be fine. I'm confident he'll be successful because he loves what he's doing, wants to remain self-employed, and has more energy than ten people put together. It just might have been less painful for him if he had taken it slower and kept it simple initially. My observation is that women are often much better at this than men, so this is a cautionary tale for the male readers of this book.

My pal Sid is another example of a late bloomer. About twelve years ago at age sixty, he closed his jewelry stores after being in retail for thirty-four years. He wisely took two years to figure out what he wanted to do next. For a whole twenty-four hours he flirted with the thought of taking a job and decided against it. In the meantime, he taught himself how to use a computer and explored how to sell on the Internet. He created a website and began promoting a special gold-plated rose, jeweled family trees, and decorative products for the home. He was excited to grow a client base that expanded from local to global. Initially, he used the basement in his house to store inventory but because his business grew so much, he moved everything into a second location. His gross revenues increased to over a million dollars a year and he has managed to continue growing his business even during the recession.

Monika began teaching Yoga in the living room of her house because as she says, "I had three boys to raise and I knew the most important job was to be able to be home to watch over those boys... who, as you know, have turned out to be wonderful functioning men, good fathers and devoted husbands."

When she moved later to a new home, she created a vibrant Yoga center and mini spa in her basement. She taught classes, sponsored guest Yoga teachers, gave therapeutic massages, and hired people to give facials. After several years, Monika felt burdened by managing all of it. In her early sixties, she decided she was ready to let it go. She closed the center, moved from the house in the suburbs into an apartment in the city, and made three decisions. First, she decided to continue to lead classes in her home but kept them small in size allowing her to have a close relationship with her students. Second, she focused on teaching Yoga for the "seasoned" body, a method she designed to meet the needs of a growing population of senior citizens. Third, she earned a current teaching certificate so she can qualify as a guest teacher at high-end resorts and in Yoga centers in other parts of the country. She loves to travel and is targeting her marketing to warmer climates where many retired people live. While she's there teaching, she'll also explore each location as a possible future home. She considers herself semi-retired and is beginning to explore her creative interest in painting and writing.

Here's one last example. Fourteen years ago, at age fifty-four, after many years as a psychotherapist, Nancy closed her practice. She was ready for a new life. She had no clear idea about what she wanted to do next, only that she wanted to continue facilitating the personal growth groups for women she had designed and been leading for years. She began exploring and was drawn to the work of Michelle Cassou, a renowned art teacher. Studying with Michelle stimulated a burst of creativity that opened up a direction for the future. Today she is still self-employed and offers services designed to enable women to find their own voice. In addition to leading personal development groups, she teaches painting from the inside out, designs and leads personal growth workshops, provides coaching for individuals, and is completing a book.

Later in life, Terry chose entrepreneurism as a new way of working and living. Sid and Monika reinvented their businesses, let go of structures they found stifling (brick and mortar), and created more freedom in their lives. Nancy changed the focus of her work but continued in a helping capacity and continued to be self-employed. All four of them took bold new risks. They have remained vital and engaged in life because their work has kept them connected to their passions and to the world around them.

In my eyes, owning a business is the best game in town, hands down. There's nothing else like it. If you're an entrepreneur, you can continue to design work and a life you love as long as you want to work.

For all your entrepreneurial life, I hope you too will say, as one of my clients did, "Life looks like I've always wanted it."

Still on Fire
(A Conclusion)

I drove to Angie's store with my heart in my throat. I knew there was a big sign in the window: "Going Out of Business. Everything Must Go." When I arrived, I was relieved to see she was busy with customers and merchandise was flying out the door. At least that will help I thought, but I was worried about her, fearing she might be depressed about closing after all her efforts to make the store a success. I'm happy to report that she looked and sounded great.

"I'm pretty sure I could have made it if I had stayed with it. I was doing better each year, but I didn't enjoy it enough to stay at it," she said. Of course she was disappointed that the store had not done better financially, but she had discovered that she didn't enjoy working in a store all day. She had felt trapped and yearned for a more flexible schedule. She acknowledged that it was time to close and felt enormous relief when she made the decision. She felt satisfied that she had given it her best effort. We both agreed that she'd earned a street MBA over the last three years. She's wiser today, vastly more experienced, and definitely not the same person she was when she started this venture.

"I thought I was my job when I left the company," she said. "Now I know I'm more than that." The brick and mortar structure of her business didn't pan out the way she had wanted but she isn't done as an entrepreneur. Months later when we met to chat, she looked healthy and happy. She has returned to using her graphic design skills, works from home, and is busy with clients, some of whom she found through the store. I doubt she will ever return to being employed. She has no regrets. "I had to do it," she said. At our meeting that day, Angie announced as she was leaving that she was on her way to a Pilates class. It was clear that her desired life style was falling into place.

My friend Sid hit a hard patch too. For the first ten years of his business, he did well and grew it rapidly. He even managed to hold his own during the worst of the recession but then he took a gamble investing a significant amount of money in some online marketing services that he hoped would expand his business significantly. They proved to be fraudulent and set him back financially in a major way. But Sid's a pro and he began immediately to redesign and rebuild his business. Recently he reported he had his biggest month ever. He added, "There is nothing like not believing the negative and believing you can... anything is possible if we get ourselves out of the way." I'm confident he'll incorporate what he learned and continue to thrive.

And after two years of being on his own, Dave decided once again that he didn't have the temperament to work alone. He's joined a small company, but this time as a partner, which allows him to remain a business owner while still being part of a team. He's continuing to do the work he loves with this company and is ecstatic. Starting his own business was the path that led him to this new venture.

Clearly, a business doesn't always work out the way you originally picture it. Sometimes it proves to be even better. And, sometimes it's disappointing. When you've had a failure, it's hard to let go of how you think it should be, but if you create a new vision that inspires you, you can get back into the game and continue to be self-employed and have a life you love. When I think about the entrepreneurial clients I've worked with, many of them in this book, I'm inspired by how well they're doing. I'm convinced they've continued to thrive even in tough times because they share nine personal qualities:

- courage
- initiative

- independence

- resilience

- flexibility

- commitment

- determination

- passion

- optimism

The list begins with *courage* because that's what it takes to leap into the unknown and meet the many challenges that will continue to arise. Successful entrepreneurs make things happen and are masterful at taking *initiative*. They don't wait to be rescued and refuse to become stuck as victims. They're *independent* and do what has to be done without someone standing over them telling them what to do.

They're *resilient* and bounce back from disappointments and setbacks, sometimes even disasters. As times and situations change, they're *flexible* and rise to the occasion by redesigning their businesses as needed. They're *committed* to being self-employed and stick with it through thick and thin. They're *determined* to do whatever it takes to be successful. They're *passionate* and are fueled by a fierce desire for freedom and love for what they're doing. And, of course, they're eternally *optimistic*, often in the face of great odds.

If you have all these qualities, you'll not only survive with a small business, but you'll thrive, keep it vibrant, and stay true to yourself in the process. I know you already have passion and optimism, maybe courage too, or you would not have picked up this book. As for the rest of these attributes, think of them as muscles. You can develop and build them as you go.

I've included exercises and action steps in the next part of this book. They correlate with the three earlier sections of the book. I'm confident they're useful. I encourage you to do those that interest you and hope you find them valuable. Use them to strengthen your resolve and hone your skills to create a vibrant small business and a life you love.

A blessing as you go forward:
May all that is unlived in you
Blossom into a future
Graced with love.

—from *To Bless the Space Between Us* by John O'Donohue

Part IV
Exercises and Suggested Action Steps

Use a journal, pad of paper, notebook, or computer to do the exercises, answer questions, and record your reflections. It will be a great roadmap.

Exercises I
Design Work and a Life You Love

Your Dream

Dreams are our guides to the future. They represent our soul's deepest longings. Do you have a dream about being self-employed and having a different life? Describe it as fully as you can. As you write, let your words flow from your heart. Remember to stay in touch with what's true for *you*, with what *you* want. Pay special attention when you feel your energy rising.

1. Describe your ideal life — a life that is exciting and inspiring. Include the following:

   a. Work – See yourself working in your own business. What is it? What are you doing?

   b. Home – Where do you live? What does it look like? Is anyone else present?

   c. Love – Fill your life with family, friends, community

   d. Play – Add adventure, silliness, hobbies

    e. Body – Incorporate exercise, food, rest, vacations

    f. Mind – How do you continue to grow and learn? Stay challenged? Books, classes, workshops?

    g. Spirit – How do you feed your soul? Church, volunteering, immersion in nature, poetry, music?

    h. Money – How much do you earn? Invest? Donate?

2. Consider this a work-in-progress. Add to it any time you think of something new. Make sure you put a date on it. It will be fun to look back on.

Fierce Desires

Fierce desire trumps fear every time. It's a powerful force that will propel you through doubts, obstacles, setbacks, and disappointments. All successful entrepreneurs are motivated by some or all of the following fierce (not lukewarm) desires for freedom. Are you?

<u>Yes</u>   <u>No</u>

I have a *fierce* desire for the freedom to:

1. Be my own boss   ____ ____

2. Set my own standards   ____ ____

3. Control my own destiny   ____ ____

4. Do things on my terms   ____ ____

5. Make my own mistakes   ____ ____

6. Have flexibility   ____ ____

7. Make my own rules   ____ ____

8. Create something of my own   ____ ____

	Yes	No
9. Do the work I want to do	___	___
10. Design my life the way I want it to be	___	___
11. Express my creativity fully	___	___
12. Make as much money as I can based on my efforts	___	___
13. Be in charge	___	___
14. Make my own decisions	___	___

What do you see about yourself? Are your desires strong enough to carry you forward?

Doubts and Fears

It's normal to have doubts and fears about stepping into self-employment but it can be paralyzing to focus on them, so just this *one time:*

1. Write down all the doubts and fears you have about being self-employed. Go ahead and whine as much as you want. Be melodramatic. Exaggerate. Go for it!

    a. Now look at your list and for each one, ask what's the worst thing that could happen?

    b. And answer, what would you do if it did?

    Okay, now focus on your strengths.

2. What are two things you've accomplished and feel great about now that were daunting or scary initially? Write a story about each in four parts:

    a. What was the challenge or problem you took on?

    b. How did you do it? What steps did you take?

    c. What did you accomplish?

    d. How did you handle your fear?

3. Think about a time when you faced a big unknown and trusted yourself. What was the situation? What decision did you make or what action did you take? What happened as a result? What did you learn?

4. What do you see about yourself from these stories? What personal qualities do you have to stand you in good stead now as you think about living your dream? List five of them:

    a. _____

    b. _____

    c. _____

    d. _____

    e. _____

5. What do you think will be your biggest pitfalls (getting side-tracked, feeling overwhelmed or lonely, working too hard, not charging enough, etc.)? List them. What ideas do you have about how you can deal with them?

Remember: courage is being afraid and doing it anyway.

The Right Time

Timing is everything and has more to do with internal readiness than external circumstances. How do you know when you're ready, especially to leave a job and move on?

Answer the following questions:

	Yes	No
1. Does your energy take a nosedive every time you think about your current job?	___	___
2. Are you bored to death in your work?	___	___
3. Do you feel unappreciated, overlooked, or underemployed?	___	___
4. Are you sick of politics and just want to focus on your work?	___	___
5. Are you restless and hungry to try something new?	___	___
6. Are you sure you will have no regrets if you leave?	___	___
7. If you were offered a new job at a different company would you refuse it?	___	___
8. If your complaints were handled at your current job, would you still want to leave?	___	___
9. Do you hear an internal voice shouting, "I am so done with this?"	___	___
10. Is fear the only thing keeping you at your job?	___	___

If you answered yes to 80% or more, get out of there as fast as you can. When you're ready internally, the business has *you* – you don't have it. Trust your intuition; it's your best friend.

Deciding What Business to Start

If you're committed to being self-employed and don't know what business you want to start, here are some exercises to stimulate ideas:

1. Answer this powerful question: What's wanted, needed, or missing that I can provide and that uses my strengths, skills, abilities, and best qualities? When these come together, that's a fit made in heaven.

2. Notice the small businesses you depend on where you live and work.

   a. Do you want to do something similar but make it better?

   b. Or, do you want to do something new, entirely different?

3. What issues, products, or services do you care about that you could build a business around?

4. What are you genuinely interested in and think you could be engaged in for a long time?

5. Clues to your passions are all around you. Pay attention to your day/night dreams, what you're drawn to, the people you hang out with, what you read, the conversations you have, and how you spend your spare time.

6. Are you already an expert in an area? What is it?

7. Because you're so good at it, what do people who love you say you should do?

8. Make a list of small businesses. Notice how many there are: financial advising/planning; pet grooming; hair salons; office/home cleaning; landscaping; massage/fitness services; retail stores; restaurants and coffee shops; management consulting; exterior/interior painting; making jewelry, etc. Any ideas?

9. Think of five specific businesses you've used and do *not* like, respect, or admire. Why?

10. Think of five specific businesses you've used and *do* like, respect, or admire. Why?

11. How do you want your business to be so that you'll like, respect, and admire it?

12. Picture yourself in your own business:

    a. What kind of business is it?

    b. What products and/or services do you offer?

    c. Where do you see yourself working? Your home? An office? A store or factory?

    d. Do you work alone or are there other people around? Who are they?

    e. Who are your customers/clients?

    f. What are your days like? How do you spend your time?

    g. How much money do you make?

    h. Anything else?

Clarifying a dream is a process, not an event. If you're still not clear about what you want to do, give yourself time. Just stay awake so you'll recognize the clues when they show up.

Good Fit Inventory

The key to being happy in your work and creating a vibrant business is to find a good fit. You know your work is an authentic self-expression when people say, "It's you!" Make sure your business idea will be based on work that:

	True	False
• You love, or are genuinely interested in	___	___
• Utilizes your strengths	___	___
• Allows you to make a difference	___	___

	True	False
• You consider a passion or calling	___	___
• You have a great time doing	___	___
• You find exciting	___	___
• You look forward to every day	___	___
• You can see yourself doing for many years	___	___
• Involves being with people you really like	___	___
• Aligns with your values	___	___
• You're eager to continue learning about	___	___
• Includes tasks you like to do	___	___
• Involves talking/reading about things that interest you	___	___
• Allows you to be authentic	___	___
• Uses your creativity and allows you to express yourself freely	___	___

What do you think? Is it a good fit?

Information Interviews

Before you take a leap into being self-employed, or if you're redesigning your business, it will be useful to conduct information interviews. Find three to five self-employed people who love being entrepreneurs and consider themselves to be successful. Do not interview people who hate their work, are struggling to survive, are cynical, or ready to quit. Try on their answers as if they were clothes. Does it sound like being an entrepreneur is a good fit for you?

Here are some suggested questions:

1. Why did you start your own business? Listen for the five fierce desires (or any others).

2. How did you decide what business to start?

3. How did you get started?

4. What do you love most about being self-employed?

5. What do like least about it?

6. What are you passionate about?

7. What need does your business fill?

8. How have you overcome fear?

9. How have you overcome obstacles?

10. What's helped you the most?

11. What did you do before you started your own business?

12. What fears did you have that never happened?

13. What difficulties have you experienced that you did not anticipate?

14. What are the good things that have surprised you?

15. What have you learned about yourself?

16. How have you grown as a person?

17. What opportunities do you have to grow or expand your business?

18. What advice do you have for me?

19. If you had to do it all over again, would you?

20. Who else should I talk to who has a business and loves it?

What did you learn about yourself from these conversations? Did you identify with the people you interviewed? With their passion?

Are you inspired and raring to go?

Your Values and Strengths

Make sure your business utilizes your strengths and lines up with your values. Then, draw on your qualities to make it happen.

1. List what you consider to be your top five strengths. Include your talents, skills, and abilities. If you're at a loss, ask your best friend, coworkers, parents, and/or spouse/live-in what they see in you.

2. List your top five values — think about the things you wouldn't do unless your life was at stake.

3. Here are the qualities I've observed in successful entrepreneurs. Check off those that apply to you:

    ____ Courageous   ____ Resilient

    ____ Creative   ____ Take initiative

    ____ Independent   ____ Generative

    ____ Committed   ____ Energetic

    ____ Flexible   ____ Enthusiastic

    ____ Passionate   ____ Determined

Four Deal-Breaking Questions

These questions are deal-breakers. If you answer "No" and cannot see a way to get past them, you will not be happy being self-employed.

	Yes	No

1. Am I okay working by myself (at least initially)?

   a. Can I work without supervision? _____ _____

   b. Can I avoid getting sidetracked by TV, kids, household tasks, etc.? _____ _____

   c. Can I keep going if I get discouraged? _____ _____

2. Can I tolerate the insecurity of an uncertain income?

   a. Can I manage to set aside money when it's flowing? _____ _____

   b. Can I draw up a budget and stick to it? _____ _____

   c. If things get tough, can I create a Plan B? _____ _____

3. Is it okay that everything depends on me?

   a. Do I prefer to make my own decisions? _____ _____

   b. Do I like being in charge? _____ _____

   c. Am I willing to take the heat if things go wrong? _____ _____

4. Can I sell myself, and my products/services?

   a. Can I present my business enthusiastically? _____ _____

   b. Can I ask for what I'm worth? _____ _____

   c. Can I get people to sign on the dotted line? _____ _____

Planning

You may not need a business plan but you do need to think through many things. Take the time to do it. Just don't get wedded to anything; your business will change in ways you can't foresee right now.

1. List all the ways you can start your business that won't have you feel paralyzed by fear. For example, brainstorm how you might line up contracts or business before you quit your job or how you can start part-time.

2. If you start a business in your home, what space will you use? How can you make it work for you?

3. Write exciting goals for your business for the next three years.

4. Next, write the steps you need to take to accomplish them.

5. List the supports you'll need — people, classes, books, workshops, etc.

6. Make a checklist of the basic things you need to get started and estimate how much they will cost. You may need some or all of the following: telephone (cell phone or landline), office rent, business cards, stationary, web site/blog, voicemail, fax, printer, computer, modem, copier, etc. If you need to carry inventory, list that too. Include the cost of a lawyer and accounting services if needed.

7. Figure out how much money you need to cover expenses for your business. Include enough for emergencies and savings if you can.

8. Figure out how much money you need to cover expenses for your personal life.

9. Total up the amount of money you have to earn to cover both business and personal expenses. Now work backwards and figure out how much you need to charge per hour/per product/

per contract to earn that amount. How many clients/companies do you need? How many days of work, etc.?

10. Create a budget for your business. Don't forget to include a category for taxes.

11. Decide on an amount you will set aside when money is flowing, not to reward yourself, but to act as a cushion when business is slow.

A Stake in the Ground

Thinking and analyzing can be paralyzing. You and everyone who loves you will be worn out if you continue to waffle. Make a commitment and take some aligned action steps. You'll unleash energy, a flow of ideas, and support.

1. Don't try to make multiple decisions at one time — e.g., Should I get married? Have a baby? Move to California? Make one decision. The rest will fall in place around it.

2. What action can you take that will deepen your commitment to your business? Rent an office? Order business cards? Etc.

3. Okay. You couldn't wait and here you are, on your own, with little or no financial cushion. Yikes! Stop planning. Get to work. Book appointments. Go get your first client/customer. Begin to discover what business you're in.

It's scary to start, but it's also exhilarating. Get your first client — you'll see!

Trust yourself. You'll figure it out as you go.

Exercises II
Adopt Powerful Practices

Selling

Without sales you have no business. The good news is that it's not an inherited gene and you can learn to be good at it. If this is a gap, just fill it.

1. Take a sales training workshop, listen to training CDs or Webinars, or read books written by experts. Or ask a friend or colleague who's good at sales to help you. Then, practice, practice, practice.

2. Set sales goals — monthly, weekly, and/or daily. Remove the mystery by figuring out how many conversations you'll need in order to generate a sale. Then be disciplined and set up that number of appointments or calls so you can reach your goals.

3. Organize the names of your contacts — how to reach them, when you last talked, the actions you took, and the outcomes. The busier you get, the more you'll need this. Follow-through makes a huge difference.

4. Learn to take the attention off yourself and put it on the people you're talking to – get interested in them. Listen, listen, listen.

Marketing

Marketing is like sowing seeds in a garden. You need patience and faith that if you keep at it regularly, you'll create results. Keep your efforts simple and do the things you enjoy so you'll be more likely to do it.

Answer these questions:

1. What do you like to do? Write? Then work on blogs, newsletters, white papers. Give talks to groups? Book presentations. Be on Facebook/ Twitter/ LinkedIn? Post to them regularly. Choose one or two methods and make it a practice. Plan to reach your prospects and clients/customers regularly, but not too often. Everyone already feels inundated with communications.

2. Write all your marketing materials in plain English. Be sure your heart is in them (not just your head) and that they reflect your personality and values.

3. Create marketing materials that are flexible and can be altered easily to meet any changes you need to make, like dates.

4. What ideas do you have to increase excellence so that clients/ customers will become raving fans and tell everyone about you?

5. Don't forget that face-to-face is still the single best way to market and sell your services. How can you get in front of people and craft conversations that open up possibilities and opportunities?

Bumps in the Road

It's inevitable that there will be times when business slows down or bad things happen. You can't manage the world; just manage yourself. Action is the best antidote to fear. Here are some suggestions:

1. When business slows down, increase your marketing efforts or dream up new products/services.

2. If it doesn't make you too anxious, rest, take a vacation, catch up on all the reading you've wanted to do, or network with lots of people before you get busy again.

3. If things get rough and you're tempted to take a job, remind yourself why you started your business in the first place.

4. If you're discouraged, conduct two kinds of information interviews:

   a. Interview people in a different business that looks easier than yours and be sure to get the real story.

   b. Interview people who have been in business for a while, are successful, and still love what they're doing. Find out how they've kept at it.

5. When the going gets tough, ask yourself this question: If I could make it work, would I keep doing this? If the answer is yes, re-commit and dig in again.

6. Remember, there's a thin line between fear and excitement. Focus on the excitement.

7. When you're in a panic, clean your closets and drawers. Nothing is more calming.

Slow Trains

Take time to work *on* your business, not just *in* it. Go somewhere other than your office — a park, library, café, or quiet room in your home. Turn off your cell phone. Do not look at emails or text messages until you have answered the following questions:

1. What areas of my business are going well?

2. What areas are not going well?

3. What ideas do I have that are exciting?

4. What supports will I need to make them happen?

5. Is there anything I've been avoiding doing?

6. What do I need/want to learn?

If you slow down long enough to think and plan, you'll shift from being reactive to proactive. You'll avoid being a victim. You'll get connected to your core vision again and rekindle inspiration.

Goals

Think of goals as an internal GPS system. Be sure to use them to motivate yourself, not as a tool for prodding or punishment. They should be a source of inspiration.

1. At least once a year, sit down and write goals for the next year, or further out.

2. Make a mini-treasure map (a small visual representation of these goals in pictures and words) to carry with you. Write your goals on the back. Be sure to look at them often.

3. If you don't meet some of your goals in one year and they still have a lot of juice for you, carry them over into the next year. Keep working on them.

4. Share your goals with people in your life who are part of your support team.

Money, Money, Money

Put practices in place to stay sane and maintain integrity.

1. Hire an accountant, even if you work by yourself. Choose someone who is honest. It's worth every penny.

2. Look at your numbers on a monthly, quarterly, and yearly basis. Don't look weekly unless you have to because you'll miss the bigger picture and end up on an emotional roller coaster. Stay conscious, not obsessed.

3. Pay your taxes on time, no matter what. No surprises, unless they're good ones, remember?

4. When you're scared about money, first calm down. Then, write down all you owe, the cash you have in the bank, and the income you project will be coming in. What's the truth? Come up with a plan for what to do. Remember, it's a better use of your time to dig deep to discover your strengths than to find a sugar daddy to rescue you.

5. In a cash-flow crisis:

   a. Come up with three (or more) ideas to generate income quickly.

   b. Come up with three (or more) ideas to generate income in the long run.

   c. Make a list of potential "angels" you can ask for a loan. A number of small loans can add up to one large loan (five friends at $10,000.00 each = $50,000.00).

6. Have you been "burned?" Put policies in place to prevent it from happening again. For example, require a down payment before you begin working on a project.

7. Is your cash/flow a disaster? Create a "cash cow" — a service or product that's not speculative, is easy to offer, and will bring in enough money so you can relax. Then concentrate on growing the rest of your business.

It's easy to make mistakes in regard to money and important to forgive yourself if you do. Mistakes are the way you learn to put good practices in place.

Money Integrity Inventory

These are good fiscal practices. Just tell the truth. Don't assume you don't need to take the inventory.

Check True or False for the following:

	True	False
1. I complete income taxes for my business on time	____	____
2. I keep track of business income on a weekly/monthly basis	____	____
3. I know where income comes from in my business	____	____
4. I have a monetary goal for this year that inspires me	____	____
5. I can see how to achieve at least 70-80% of this goal	____	____
6. I pay quarterly taxes on time	____	____
7. I have a separate bank account for my business	____	____
8. I use Quicken (or some other method) to keep track of finances	____	____

9. I have a separate credit card for
   my business   ____   ____

10. I keep receipts for business expenses   ____   ____

11. I record all out-of-pocket expenses and
    reimburse myself   ____   ____

12. I charge enough for my services/products   ____   ____

13. I earn enough to have the lifestyle I want   ____   ____

14. I have no credit card debt (or am reducing
    it regularly)   ____   ____

15. I record all cash transactions   ____   ____

16. I'm current with business   ____   ____

17. I reward myself with money, time off,
    and vacations   ____   ____

18. I use an accountant to help with taxes,
    payroll, etc.   ____   ____

19. I know what is most profitable in
    my business   ____   ____

20. I'm saving money for down times   ____   ____

21. I'm saving money for "retirement"   ____   ____

22. I have a budget and use it as a guide   ____   ____

23. I put money aside for payroll taxes and do
    not dip into it   ____   ____

When you're scared about money, first calm down. Then, from a more peaceful place, you can figure out how much you need to curb your panic and what your next steps should be.

Exercises III
Learn the Art of Thriving

Well Being

You are the heart and soul of your business. It's a wise investment to take good care of yourself. Too much work and no play is not healthy. It skews your perspective.

1. Take one full day a week off, no matter what.

2. Pace yourself and build in breaks during the day.

3. Stay sober and clean. Overuse of drugs and alcohol (any risky behavior) will undermine your efforts. Even watch your caffeine intake — don't add to your stress level.

4. Put an exercise plan in place. Walk, swim, run, ride a bike, lift weights, do core body exercises — whatever works for you. Schedule it regularly. If you need to, find a buddy to do it with you — you'll be more likely to follow through.

5. Add an activity for flexibility — Yoga, dance, etc. Schedule that too.

6. Incorporate practices that feed your soul and are a good fit — praying, chanting, attending religious services, spending time in nature, listening to great music, reading poetry, etc.

7. Read inspiring books, listen to motivating CDs, watch uplifting movies/DVDs.

8. Attend workshops on personal growth, not just business.

9. Set boundaries for your work — times to end the day, weekend time off, etc. Announce these boundaries and be vigilant about protecting them. Being successful doesn't depend on non-stop work as much as on being smart. Honor your well-being. Remember: you became an entrepreneur in order to have a whole life.

Support

Even if you work alone, it's hard (if not impossible) to do it by yourself. It's not weak to ask for help; it's smart.

1. Find or start a group with other entrepreneurs. Use a facilitator/coach to manage the group, especially if there's any danger of it turning into a "pity party" (see guidelines that follow).

2. Get out of the office often and meet with people. Have coffee, lunch, etc. Make sure you're with upbeat people who are positive and optimistic.

3. Volunteer for a cause you're passionate about. You'll meet new people and feel more connected with your community, whether it's where you live or work. You'll gain perspective, take your mind off work, and feel like a whole human being.

4. Hire some help. No one can do everything well, even you. Do what you do best and give/delegate the rest of it. Someone helping even a few hours a week will make a big difference.

5. Spend time doing things you love outside of work.

Don't let yourself get isolated. Make sure you don't get stuck in your own ruts.

Guidelines for Forming an Entrepreneurs' Support Group

These are the things I've learned that foster a successful group:

1. One person has to be responsible for the group and facilitate the meetings. His/her job is to "hold the space" (set meeting dates, send email reminders, tend to everyone in the group during and after meetings, and continue to enroll members when needed). It's critical that the leader is also a business owner.

2. Keep the group small – 6 to 8 members works best so everyone has time to talk.

3. Schedule three hours. Allow each person about twenty minutes and use a timer.

4. No one should have a competing business although I allow members to be in the same genre as long as they have a different focus and client/customer base. Every member should be earning a living as an entrepreneur. I do not allow people to join the group who work for companies – e.g., insurance or real estate sales.

5. I require every member to commit to the group for six months. I do not let people observe or attend once "to see what it's like" because it's a personal, intimate group. Of course, if someone is unhappy after the first time or it's clear that it's a bad fit, it's best not to continue. I also let people stay as long as they want to (sometimes years and years) as long as they're actively working on their business and not just socializing.

6. I prefer a relaxed setting. I do not recommend a restaurant unless it's self-serve – too much attention on food, confusion about who pays what, no privacy. I like using the living room in my home. Providing coffee and food is optional (I like doing it). Water is really all that's needed because many people bring their own drink concoctions anyway and others are watching their weight. I allow people to arrive fifteen minutes early to chat, have coffee, and settle in.

7. I start the group with a short, closed-eye meditation to help people get centered and present. I ask them to think about all the accomplishments they've had since we last met and to choose one to talk about. Then I ask them to think about the challenges ahead and choose one to work on. I urge them to make sure they get what they want and need in the meeting so they can leave inspired and ready to get into action.

8. Be sure everyone starts a check-in with an accomplishment. Don't let people go immediately into their concerns. This is very important, for them and for you.

9. Always allow people to talk about life issues if they pertain to work. If something comes up that's not appropriate for the group, encourage that member to seek help for that elsewhere. As an example someone might be struggling with an unhappy marriage. You can point out the cost to their business and well-being but then urge them to see a psychotherapist.

10. Build trust in the group by asking for confidentiality and openly sharing your failures, mistakes, and the lessons you've learned. Express encouragement, compassion, and confidence in each member.

11. Challenge each member to be his/her best. Be willing to confront behavior that's getting in the way of success. Listen for the music (not the words) and get to the heart of the matter instead of focusing on surface issues. Sometimes a dose of tough love is needed – create a positive context first, make sure you come from your heart, and do laser surgery.

12. Ask for promises for the next month and remind people about them at the next meeting if needed (I take notes). Ask members who have not kept their word what they did accomplish because often they've done a lot, just not what they planned to do. Check to see if they still want to work on their promises. If they break them repeatedly, this is the time to confront them about this and explore what's going on.

13. Let people go when it's clearly the right time for them to leave. I request that members announce their plan to leave a month in advance and then at their last meeting, reflect on where they were when they joined, what they've accomplished since then, and what supports they have in place to move forward. This is the ideal way to do it but it doesn't always work out because life is usually messier than that. When it's done right, it's great for them and everyone else. It allows for a good completion.

14. I send an email out to everyone after each meeting summarizing the meeting and adding any new thoughts I have for each member. I request that absent members send a summary by email to all the group members in order to remain in the loop. (No more than two absences every six months if possible).

15. I bill people quarterly.

16. Sometimes we have a topic we discuss before we begin with individual check-ins, e.g., what having integrity in your business looks like, or what the new reality means for your business. Members like these discussions. They're lively and interesting.

17. This is not a networking or leads group, although that often happens naturally. Create a group where members can: brainstorm, discover contacts and resources, be listened to, find creative solutions, receive feedback on plans and marketing materials, figure things out as they talk, test ideas, celebrate successes, mourn failures, and get pumped up all over again.

18. I only invite entrepreneurs who have small businesses since that's what I know best.

19. If you're the leader, make sure you get inspired too, have a lot of fun, and love the members.

Perks

Be the boss you would want. Be good to yourself and enjoy all the stellar perks of being self-employed.

1. If you haven't scheduled a vacation for this year, do it now. If you can, make it for more than two weeks.

2. If you need a sabbatical, plan it and put it in your schedule. Yes, a sabbatical (any amount of time from one month to a year). Delicious!

3. If you absolutely can't get away for a long time, add extra days on to holiday weekends — four days off rather than three. If it's slow for you between Christmas and New Year's, close down and relax.

4. Sign up for a class or workshop you're itching to take. Enter it in your appointment system.

5. Schedule appointments (haircuts, medical and dental check-ups, etc.) and tasks (grocery shopping, errands, etc.) during the week instead of on the weekend. You'll get them done faster and avoid long lines.

6. Go to your children's events.

7. Plan your day around time with your family.

Authentic Choices

You'll have to make many decisions in the life of your business. Some will have a big impact – like moving your office outside your home or taking on a partner. Be thoughtful as you make them and make sure they reflect who you are. Don't give in to ego-driven concerns.

1. What decisions are you confronting? (Re-locating your office, hiring employees, taking on a partner, expanding or growing, etc.). Write them down.

2. What consequences do you foresee from your decisions?

3. On a scale of 1 to 10, rate each decision. 1 = I hate this but I don't see any other possibility; 5 = I'm okay with this; 10 = I'm motivated by this.

4. Still not sure? Ask yourself if you're listening to your heart or your ego. Try to separate the two. List the reasons for your decisions under each heading.

5. Remember information interviews? This is a good time to interview people who seem happy with the decisions they've made in similar situations. As you listen, try on their solutions but remember, the best advisor is *you*.

Wisdom resides in your heart, not your ego. It takes courage and strength to honor your heart, but it will prove to be a good guide in the long run and will support your authenticity.

Fully Engaged

If you're feeling bored, burned out, or disengaged, take time to figure out what's missing. How did your business lose its vibrancy – what happened, not who is to blame? How did you lose a life you loved? How can you recreate that, or design something new that's right for you at this time in your life?

Go somewhere quiet to answer these questions:

1. If you could have your work/life be any way you wanted it right now, what would it look like?

2. What could be motivating, exciting, inspiring to you now, at this point in your life?

3. Is there something you've always wanted to do?

4. What would be a new expression for your business that would re-engage you?

It's probably not a question of whether you want to remain self-employed; it's about what to do next to feel invigorated all over again.

Late Blooming

The best thing about having your own business is that you can work as much or as little as you want, for as long as you want. Don't let societal prejudices and misinformation about aging and retirement get in the way.

1. Look around. Notice older people who are happily self-employed.

2. What could you do that would add spice to your life and allow you to blossom fully? Write it down.

   a. Now write all the reasons why you think you can't do it.

   b. Now write all the reasons why you think you can do it.

3. Get going. Take the first steps.

Take a chance on yourself. Working is a way to stay connected to life and some of your best work may happen in your later years.

This life is not a dress rehearsal.

An Eclectic Recommended Reading List

A Whole New Mind and *Drive* by Daniel Pink

Book Yourself Solid by Michael Port

EQ by Daniel Goleman

Growing a Business by Paul Hawkens

Finding Meaning in the Second Half of Life by James Hollis

Happier by Tal Ben-Shahar

Learned Optimism and *Flourish* by Martin Seligman

Let Your Life Speak by Parker Palmer

Lost and Found by Geneen Roth

Outliers by Malcolm Boyd

Rework by Jason Fried and David Heinemeier Hansso

Six Months Off by Hope Dlugozima, James Scott, and David Sharp

Starting Your Own Business by Jan Norman

The 4-Hour Work Week by Timothy Ferriss

The Power of Full Engagement by Jim Loehr and Tony Schwartz

The Seven Habits of Highly Effective People by Stephen Covey

The Toilet Paper Entrepreneur by Mike Michalowicz

Tribes by Seth Godin

Gratitude

Thank you to each one of all the people who have participated in my entrepreneurs' groups over the years. You're my heroes and heroines. I've been inspired by your courage and successes. Thank you especially to long-time and current members: Bobbye, Colin, Monika, John, Rose, Stephanie, Jennifer, Jane, Melissa, Pam, Keith, Arnie, Bruce, Terry, Sheryl, Julia, Vickie, and Tom.

This book would not have happened without a village of support. Thank you, Nancy Hill. You've been a friend and writing partner for so many years I can't remember when we first met. We're in each other's DNA. BWFF. I love you and thank you for your unrelenting commitment to my best self, your wisdom, humor, and your gorgeous writing. Thank you, Monica Paxson. We created a writing group over fifteen years ago and have remained friends ever since. Thank goodness you're in my life. Without your brilliance, creativity, and vision, I might still be whining and stuck in the 20th Century. Thank you, Cathy Mauk, for keeping our connection alive over thousands of miles. I appreciate your intellect, lyrical descriptions of place, wise recommendations, and your "by-god-we're-going-to do-it" commitment to writing.

Thank you, Natalie Goldberg, for creating wonderful writing workshops that ignited a love affair with writing and opened new friendships with fellow travelers on this path. Thank you, Tania Casselle and Sean Murphy, for being superb teachers with generous, loving hearts. Thank you, Cindy Crosby, for your continued help and faith in me. Thank you, Joe Durepos, for challenging me in a way that brought out the tiger and helped me find a place to stand. Thank you, Bret Nicholaus, for your generous encouragement. You're a wonderful role model. Thank you, Jessie Kirchoff, for holding my hand at a Taos Writing Conference and encouraging me to keep going with the mish mash I showed up with years ago.

Thank you, Rich Lessor, my colleague, cheerleader, and guru for over twenty years. What would I do without you? Get into trouble, for sure.

Thank you to the participants in my writing support groups — for trusting me, being vulnerable, and sharing your writing. Your courage and commitment is inspiring: Rose Mattax, Bruce Hodes, Wendy Tynan, Gail Cowan, Pam Wilfong, Laura McAlpine, Lorna

Thrive

Sullivan, David Beleckis, Margaret Burk, Lupe Wood, and Kathy Flanagan.

Thank you Michael Reed, Colin Reed, SuAnne Lawrence, Pam Winkler, Sally Simmel, and JoAnne Cimbalo for following the progress of this book, taking time to hear and read parts, and listening. You've always given honest, thoughtful feedback, encouraged me to stay true to myself, and kept me going. Everyone needs good friends like you. Thank you, Gary Mitchiner, for your belief in me and for brilliant advice. Thank you, Becky Doar, for your generous help and the gift of an eagle eye.

Thank you, Mary Lostarakos and Quinessa Solomon for your presence in my life. When you show up, it's like opening a window and letting in the sun. Mary, a special thank you for your generosity and for how calmly and effortlessly you handle everything. Q, you're an old soul, wise beyond your years in both mind and spirit.

Thank you to my family for caring about me and always being in my corner: Ben and Judy, Brian and Mary Jo, David and Mary Jo.

Most of all, thank you Earl. You're the solid foundation in my life. Nobody could be luckier than I am to have you as my husband. Thank you for believing in me and loving me.

Made in the USA
Charleston, SC
22 July 2012